About This Book 4
Links to the Language Arts Standards 5
25 Spelling Stumpers Mini-Poster 8

Chapter 1: Sneaky Sound Patterns
(Alternate Spellings of Letter Sounds) 9
The Knight's Knot /n/ sound 10
Tough Enough! Crossword /f/ sound 12
"J" Jars /j/ sound 13
Write These Words! Flip Book /r/ sound 15
Climb Aboard! /m/ sound 17
Spelling Snake /s/ sound 18
Vowel Tic-Tac-Toe
long-*o*, -*e*, and -*a* sounds 19

Chapter 2: Which One (Won) Is It?
(Homophones) 24
Which Word? 25
Homophone Cupboard Mini-Book 26
Their, *They're*, or *There*? 29
The To-Too-Two Square 30

Chapter 3: Putting Together Words
(Compound Words and Contractions) 33
Build-a-Word Crossword Puzzle 35
Flower Power 36
Contraction Action Card Game 38
Calling All Contractions! 41
The "NOT" Spot Spinner Game 42

Chapter 4: Rules Rule!
(Plurals and Past-Tense Verbs) 45
Sammy's Eight Days of Camping
Plurals Mini-Book 46
Crack the Plurals Code! 50
Spell-the-Past-Tense-Perfectly! Word Search 51
Greetings From Camp Spelli-Melli!
Past-Tense Slider 52
I Before *E* Mini-Book 56
Presto Change-o! With -*ing* 59

Chapter 5: No Rules Here!
(Irregular Verbs) 60
Past-Tense Parade Board Game 61
Spelling Skylines 64
Be a News Editor! 65

Chapter 6: Spelling Stumpers
(Spelling Aids and Strategies) 66
Tips From Top Spellers 67
Sign-Language Spelling 68
Personal Pocket Dictionary 70
Spelling CPR Study Aid 72
Make a Mnemonic! 75
Confusing Words Cube 76

Answers 78

Additional Spelling Resources 80

About This Book

A lot has changed in spelling instruction over the past few decades. When I was in school, spelling was reserved for Friday mornings, when we would be quizzed on a list of words we had memorized the night before. And except for the occasional spelling bee, spelling was never exactly what I would call fun.

Today many teachers are working to make spelling instruction more authentic and enjoyable. They celebrate the natural link between spelling and writing and acknowledge that it does not matter if a student can score 100 on a spelling test if she can't spell words correctly in a letter or story. This book is designed to help teachers in that important mission. You'll find spelling strategies and activities to reach students of every learning style. These include mini-books, manipulatives, puzzles, poems, and games that will help kids remember hundreds of hard-to-spell words.

Why Does Spelling Matter?

Some argue that spelling instruction is nearly obsolete in this age of computerized spell check. They could not be more wrong. No one can have a computer handy all the time—and even when one is working at a computer, spell-check programs rarely catch every mistake. Although they are helpful, spell-check programs frequently fail to find errors in usage of homophones such as *deer/dear*, *to/two/too*, and *their/they're/there*. My own spell check changes my last name, "Kellaher," to *Kalahari* (the African desert) each time it encounters it! When such spelling errors make it into the final draft of a piece of writing, it's the writer—not the computer—who appears disorganized and inattentive.

Of course, spelling is not the single most important element in written communication. Ideas should always come first. That's why most teachers choose to let students use invented spelling in the very early grades. If we told children that they could only use words they knew they could spell correctly, we would virtually guarantee bad writing! (We would also have a great many children who couldn't bear to put pen to paper.)

However, there's no doubt about it: Spelling *does* matter. Regardless of their language arts philosophy, all teachers eventually expect students to hand in polished pieces of writing—complete with properly spelled words. By the second grade, correcting one's spelling should be a standard part of the writing process. And spelling instruction—that is, helping students uncover rules and strategies to enable them to spell words correctly—should be part of the curriculum.

Spelling Secrets

BY KAREN KELLAHER

SCHOLASTIC
PROFESSIONAL BOOKS

NEW YORK • TORONTO • LONDON • AUCKLAND • SYDNEY
MEXICO CITY • NEW DELHI • HONG KONG • BUENOS AIRES

To Liza Charlesworth and Deborah Schecter,

two amazing editors.

Liza, enjoy the exciting new chapter in your life!

Cover artwork by Jared Lee
Cover design by Josué Castilleja
Interior artwork by Mike Moran, except pages 11 and 69 by Maxie Chambliss
Interior design by Kathy Massaro
ISBN: 0-439-37073-6

1 2 3 4 5 6 7 8 9 10 40 09 08 07 06 05 04 03

Why Do Some Students Struggle With Spelling?

Mastering spelling can be difficult in a language with so many rules—*and* exceptions to those rules! English words that sound alike often have completely different spellings. While reading voraciously from an early age seems to boost spelling skills, even avid readers and writers can stumble over these complexities.

Although it's easy to shrug and conclude that some students are natural-born spellers while others simply are not, the truth is that effective spellers usually have tricks they use to learn and memorize correct spellings. These tricks—such as inventing spelling jingles and creating personal dictionaries—can help all students become better spellers. In this book I will introduce some basic spelling rules and provide plenty of fun tricks and spelling strategies for you to share with students.

Using This Book

Each chapter in this book focuses on a potential spelling trouble spot: sneaky sound patterns, homophones, compound words and contractions, rules for spelling regular plurals and past-tense verbs, and tips for spelling irregular verbs. There's also a chapter chock-full of suggestions for mastering demon words. (Everybody has a few of those; my own worst spelling stumper is *accommodate*!)

You may choose to use the activities in the order in which they appear, or hop around to suit your students' needs. I recommend sharing with students the purpose of each activity before you begin. You'll find the main spelling focus at the top of each activity. Say, for example, "In this activity, we are going to look at some different ways of spelling the /f/ sound. What are some ways to spell that sound?" By sharing the goal of the activity from the very beginning, you'll help students understand the context for the work they are about to do.

Keep in mind that while the activities in this book can be used for whole-class exercises, many can also be used for independent work. Because different students face different spelling challenges, you might consider creating a Spelling Skills Corner in your classroom. Stock it with copies of your favorite activities (choose several from each chapter), some dictionaries, and pencils. When students finish work early or need extra review in a specific spelling skill, invite them to visit the Spelling Skills Corner and choose an activity to try.

Links to the Language Arts Standards

The activities in this book are aligned with the following language arts standards outlined by the Mid-Continent Regional Educational Laboratory (MCREL), an organization that collects and synthesizes noteworthy national and state K–12 curriculum standards.

Uses conventions of spelling in written compositions:

- spells high frequency, commonly misspelled words from appropriate grade-level list
- uses a dictionary and other resources to spell words
- uses initial consonant substitution to spell related words
- uses vowel combinations for correct spelling
- uses contractions, compounds, roots, suffixes, prefixes, and syllable constructions to spell words

Source: *A Compendium of Standards and Benchmarks for K–12 Education* (Mid-Continent Regional Educational Laboratory, 1995)

Spelling Stumpers Mini-Poster

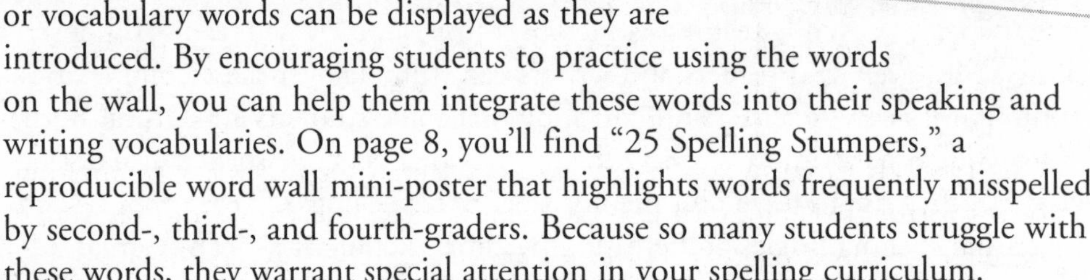

You and your students may already be familiar with the concept of a word wall, a wall or other special place in the classroom where new spelling or vocabulary words can be displayed as they are introduced. By encouraging students to practice using the words on the wall, you can help them integrate these words into their speaking and writing vocabularies. On page 8, you'll find "25 Spelling Stumpers," a reproducible word wall mini-poster that highlights words frequently misspelled by second-, third-, and fourth-graders. Because so many students struggle with these words, they warrant special attention in your spelling curriculum.

Of course, not every hard-to-spell word is listed on the mini-poster. For example, I deliberately did not include many homophones—words that sound the same but have different spellings and meanings. (There are so many tricky homophones that I gave these words their own chapter, complete with activities to help students put the words in context.) However, you'll find that the words on the poster are ones students use most often in their writing and struggle to spell correctly.

To make the most of the mini-poster, try some or all of the following suggestions:

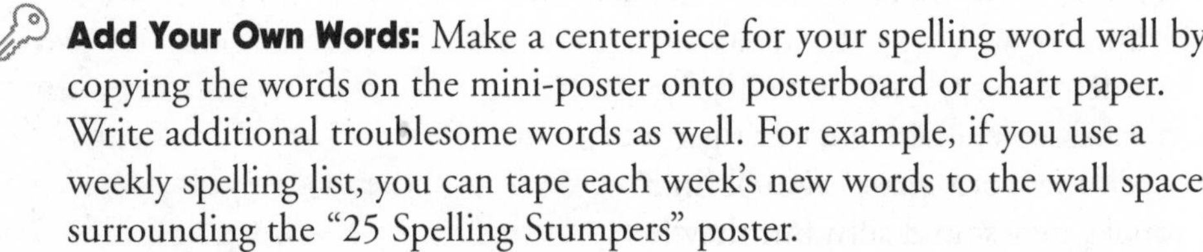

Add Your Own Words: Make a centerpiece for your spelling word wall by copying the words on the mini-poster onto posterboard or chart paper. Write additional troublesome words as well. For example, if you use a weekly spelling list, you can tape each week's new words to the wall space surrounding the "25 Spelling Stumpers" poster.

Play With the Words: Use riddles to encourage students to interact with the mini-poster. Say, for example, "I am thinking of a word that has a silent *e* and means to choose." (*decide*) Or "I am thinking of a word that sounds like it should be spelled *d-u-z*." (*does*) Ask that students respond with both the word and its correct spelling. You can even turn this into a game show with small prizes! As an alternative, have students follow specific instructions to build mini word lists from the poster. For example, instruct students to list all the words on the word wall that have a silent *e*. Other instructions might include:

- List all the words that have vowel blends.
- List.all the words that start with a vowel.
- List all the words that end in a consonant.
- List all the words that have the long-*a* sound.
- List all the words that have two syllables.

By reviewing the words over and over again and writing down those that match your criteria, students will become familiar with the words.

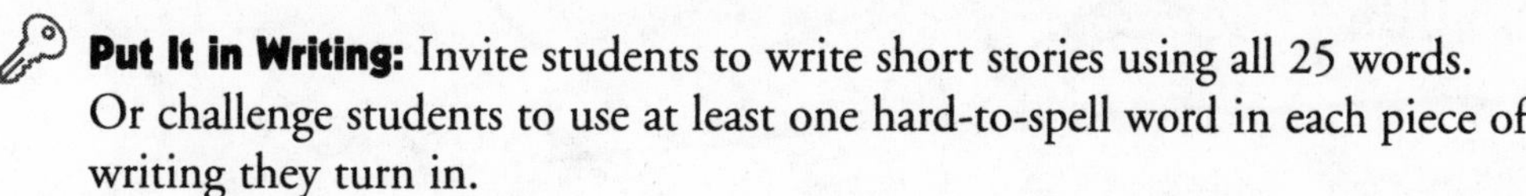

Put It in Writing: Invite students to write short stories using all 25 words. Or challenge students to use at least one hard-to-spell word in each piece of writing they turn in.

Have a Word Hunt: Hide some or all of the words in a word-search puzzle. Make words go across, down, or on the diagonal. Searching for the words will reinforce correct spellings.

Chant It Out: Rhythm and repetition are wonderful tricks for remembering how to spell challenging words. Each day, choose one word from the wall to chant or cheer together. For example, you can use this old cheerleading cry with any word you like:

Give me an A.	"A!"
Give me a G.	"G!"
Give me an A.	"A!"
Give me an I.	"I!"
Give me an N.	"N!"
What does it spell?	"Again!"

You might also try having kids shout out the spelling of a word while touching their toes for each letter (this way, you'll get students' blood pumping while giving them a fun way to memorize the spelling). Or invite students to spell words aloud together using a variety of funny voices. Say, for example, "Let's use our tiger voices this time" or "Let's whisper while we spell the word *quiet.*" (You'll find other ideas in the box below.) These little tricks may sound silly, but they help students find a hook in their memories on which to hang the difficult word. The next time students need to remember the spelling of the word, they might just hear that tiger voice or that whisper in the back of their minds!

Say It This Way:

- Spell the word while holding your nose.
- Sing the letters out like an opera singer might.
- Use sign language letters to spell the word (see page 68).
- Say the letters as if you are calling out winning lottery numbers.
- Spell it with an exaggerated accent.
- Say the spelling very slowly, stretching out each letter.

stink

Kids' Page

25 Spelling Stumpers

These words can be tough to spell! Use this word wall to check your spelling when you edit your writing. Add your own spelling stumpers at the end of the list.

again	favorite	until
almost	friend	upon
always	laugh	were
answer	people	women
because	quiet	would
believe	really	________
chocolate	said	________
decide	special	________
different	surprise	________
does	tomorrow	________

Sneaky Sound Patterns

(Alternate Spellings of Letter Sounds)

Explore words with confusing consonant blends and tricky vowel combinations.

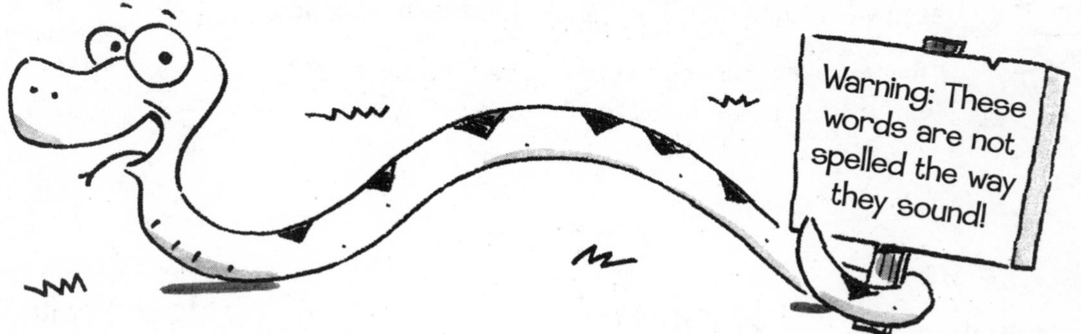

When children are learning to read unfamiliar words, one task they perform is to connect speech sounds to the letters and groups of letters on the page. They then blend the speech sounds together (and, of course, use context clues) to read the word. In theory, learning to spell is simply the reciprocal of this process. A student says or hears a word, identifies the distinct speech sounds that make up the word, then writes the letters and groups of letters that represent those sounds.

If life were fair, spelling would always work this way! We would hear the /n/ sound and confidently write the letter *n* instead of wondering if the word might be spelled with a *kn* as in *know* or a *gn* as in *gnome*. We would not have half a dozen choices for spelling the long-*a* sound (for example, *cake*, *neighbor*, *May*, *bait*)!

But we all know that life is not fair—and that English can be one of the most confusing languages in the world. Many words are not spelled the way they sound. That's why your students must move beyond phonetic spelling and explore the unusual spelling patterns that can trip them up.

In this chapter you'll find activities to help students explore and remember words that use alternate or unusual spellings for familiar sounds, including:

- words that use *kn* instead of *n*
- words that use alternate spellings of the /f/ sound (*gh* and *ph*)
- words that use all variations of the /j/ sound (*j*, *g*, and *dge*)
- words that use *wr* instead of *r*
- words that use *mb* instead of *m*
- words that use all variations of the /s/ sound
- words that use all spellings of the long-vowel sounds

Name ______________________

Date ______________________

Alternate spellings of the /n/ sound

The Knight's Knot

PART 1

Some words use the letters *kn* to make the /n/ sound. Unscramble each *kn* word in the list below, then match each word to its meaning. We did the first one for you.

Then read the story on the next page. Choose a word from the list to fill in each blank in the story.

Spelling Secret

Remember that only a handful of words use *kn* to make the /n/ sound. When you see them, you'll notice that the letters *kn* are usually at the beginning of the word.

(1) **GHNKIT**	knight	to sew with yarn
(2) **EWKN**	______	pounded on a door
(3) **KENE**	______	a brave character from a fairy tale
(4) **TOKN**	______	realized or thought
(5) **IFKNE**	______	the handle on a door
(6) **CDKNKEO**	______	something you tie with a shoelace
(7) **BONK**	______	a sharp tool used to cut food
(8) **TINK**	______	part of your leg

Kids' Page

Name ______________________ Date ______________

The Knight's Knot

Part 2

Once upon a time, a wise princess lived in a castle far, far away. She loved to read and ______________ sweaters. Many young men wished to marry the princess, but the princess ______________ they were not right for her. She said she would marry only the smartest, kindest man in the kingdom.

To find her true love, the princess wrapped a magic rope around the castle and tied it in a strong ______________ . She announced that the man who could untie the rope would win her hand in marriage and all the gold in the kingdom.

Many men tried to untie the rope. A handsome prince tugged on the rope with all his might. A farmer tried to cut the rope with his ______________ . Nothing worked.

One day a brave ______________ came to the castle. He got down on one ______________ and ______________ on the castle door. When the princess turned the ______________ and opened the door, the brave man spoke. "I have heard of your great kindness and wisdom," he said. "I do not need all the gold in the kingdom. I want only the treasure of your company."

The princess was moved by the man's kind words. So was the rope! As the man spoke, the knot magically came untied. And from that moment on, the two lived happily ever after.

The End

Name ________________________________

Date ________________________________

Alternate spellings of the /f/ sound

Tough Enough!

Some words use the letters *ph* or *gh* to make the /f/ sound. First, study the words in the Word Box. Add the letters *ph* or *gh* to complete each word. Then use the words to solve each crossword puzzle clue. Write your answers in the puzzle.

Spelling Secret

The letters *ph* make the /f/ sound at the beginning, middle, or end of a word. The letters *gh* can only make the /f/ sound when they appear at the middle or end of a word.

Word Box

tou ___ ___	___ ___ oto	gra ___ ___	___ ___ one	___ ___ ilip
lau ___ ___	rou ___ ___	cou ___ ___	enou ___ ___	geogra ___ ___ y

Crossword Clues

ACROSS

4. I hear the _______ ringing.
5. I wish someone would _______ at my jokes.
6. In school, we made a _______ of our favorite pets.
9. Our class _______ was taken today.

DOWN

1. We brought _______ snacks for everyone.
2. The waves were too _______ for swimming.
3. My _______ book has a good map of the United States.
4. My brother's name is _______ .
7. The math test was really _______ .
8. A cold can make you sneeze and _______ .

"J" Jars

Use with Kids' Page 14.

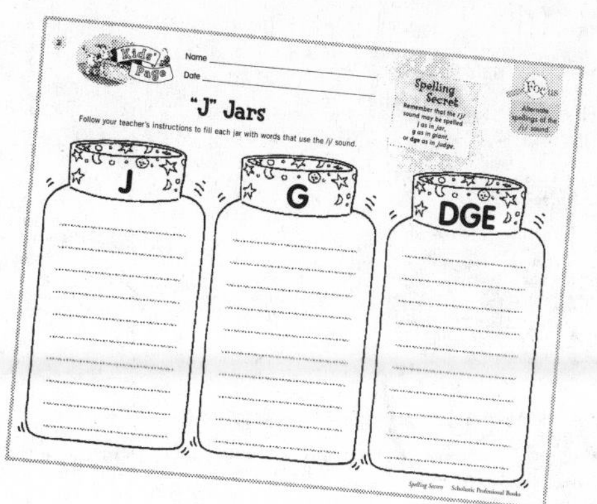

On the reproducible that follows, students explore the various spellings of the /j/ sound: *j* as in *jar*, *g* as in *giant*, and *dge* as in *judge*. There are two variations of this spelling activity. Choose the one that best matches your students' skill level.

Variation 1: Freestyle

Invite students to brainstorm words that use the /j/ sound and to jot the words down in the appropriate jars on the reproducible. Afterward, compile students' individual lists into three master lists (you can even draw three large jars on the board). See how many words students came up with for each spelling of the /j/ sound. Ask: "Which spelling seems to be most common?" (*the* j *spelling*) "Which spelling never appears at the beginning of a word?" (*the* dge *spelling*)

Variation 2: Teacher-Guided

Instead of having students come up with words on their own, read aloud a prepared list of familiar words that use the /j/ sound (see list below). Read one word at a time, then use it in a sentence. Instruct students to write each word in the appropriate jar. When you have finished the list, check to see that students have spelled the words correctly. For each word, ask: "Which jar did you place this word in? Can you spell the word aloud for the class?"

Point out that the word *judge* can be placed in both the "J" jar and the "DGE" jar, since it uses both spellings.

Word List for "J" Jars

jam	job	jump
giant	judge	junior
engine	Jill	Jupiter
joke	subject	fudge
gentle	ledge	genius
budge	germ	edge
Jim	jar	jelly

Alternate spellings of the /j/ sound

Challenge students to make a bar graph showing the number of words they uncovered that use each spelling of the /j/ sound. Try conducting the same activity with other sounds for which there are alternate spellings, such as the /f/ sound (*f, gh,* and *ph*); the /k/ sound (*k, c, ck,* and *ch*) or the long-*a* sound (*a, ai, ey*). By graphing the various spellings, students will learn which spellings are most and least common.

Kids' Page

Name ______________________

Date ______________________

"J" Jars

Spelling Secret

Remember that the /j/ sound may be spelled **j** as in *jar*, **g** as in *giant*, or **dge** as in *judge*.

Focus

Alternate spellings of the /j/ sound

Follow your teacher's instructions to fill each jar with words that use the /j/ sound.

J

G

DGE

Write These Words! Flip Book

Use with Kids' Page 16.

The *wr* spelling of the /r/ sound is not a particularly common one. It is also a spelling pattern that many young students have difficulty remembering. For example, many second-, third-, and fourth-graders habitually spell *write* as *rite.* In this flip-book activity, students will get to know eight frequently used words that use the *wr* blend.

You Will Need

- copies of Kids' Page 16
- scissors
- stapler
- markers
- pencils

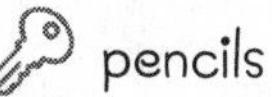

Alternate spellings of the /r/ sound

Making the Flip Books

1 Provide each student with a copy of the reproducible. Ask students to cut out the rectangle and square shapes along the dotted lines.

2 Tell students to set aside the squares with the bird (wren) and wrist. They should also set aside the two blank word-ending squares. These four squares will be used at the end of the activity.

3 Have students look at each picture square and ask themselves what *wr* word it represents. Demonstrate how to find the word-ending square that forms that word. For example, after studying the picture of the wrench, students will look for the square with the ending *-ench* and place it to the right of the letters *wr* in order to form that word on the flip book rectangle.

4 One by one, have students match the pictures and word endings in corresponding piles on the flip book.

5 When students have finished, call their attention to the two picture squares they set aside in step 2. Ask: "What *wr* word does this picture show?" Let students consult a children's dictionary if they are unsure. When they have identified the words *wrist* and *wren,* invite them to write the endings for these words on the blank word-ending squares.

6 Then direct them to add the two new words to the top of the flip book. Affix the picture squares and word ending squares to the rectangle by stapling along the top edge of each pile.

7 Have students use the *wr* words from the flip book in their writing. You can have students write an original sentence for each word or combine the words in a short story or rap song.

Invite students to use a dictionary to come up with additional frequently used words that start with *wr.* Some examples include: *wrestling, wristwatch, wreath, wriggle, wretched,* and *wrapper.*

wr

Write These Words! Flip Book

		ite	eck
		ench	inkled
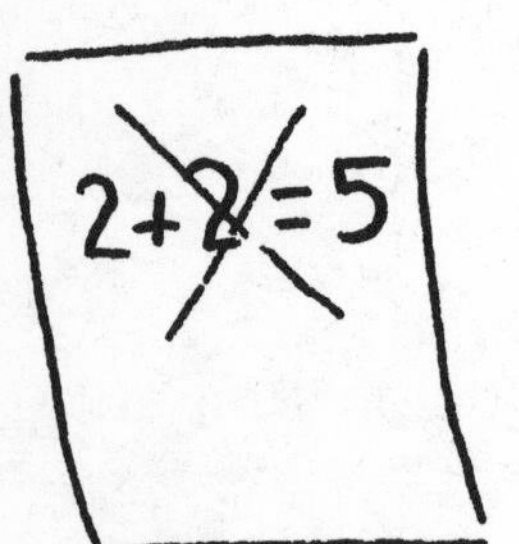		ong	apped
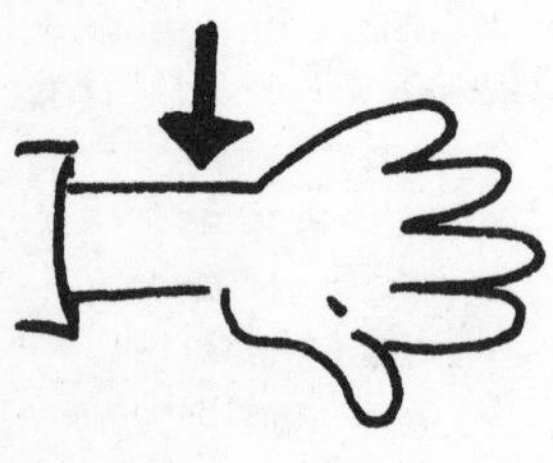			

Name ______________________________

Date ______________________________

Climb Aboard!

In a few words, the letters *m* and *b* join together to make the /m/ sound. The poor *b* loses its sound altogether! Read the sentences below, and choose a word from the Word Box to fill in the blank. Then circle your answers in the train engine puzzle. Words can go across or down.

Spelling Secret

Memorize this sentence to remember some words that use *mb* to spell the /m/ sound:
The *lamb climbed* away from the fold until its *limbs* grew *numb* with cold.

1. A ________________ is a baby sheep.
2. You must ________________ to get to the top of a mountain.
3. You can use a ________________ to make your hair look neat.
4. When you can't feel anything, you are ________________ .
5. You might find a ________________ on top of a grave.
6. An arm is an example of a ________________ .

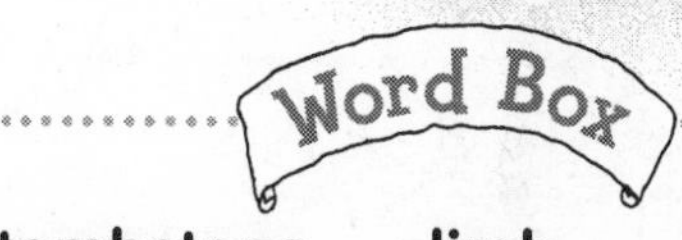

tombstone	**limb**	**lamb**
comb	**numb**	**climb**

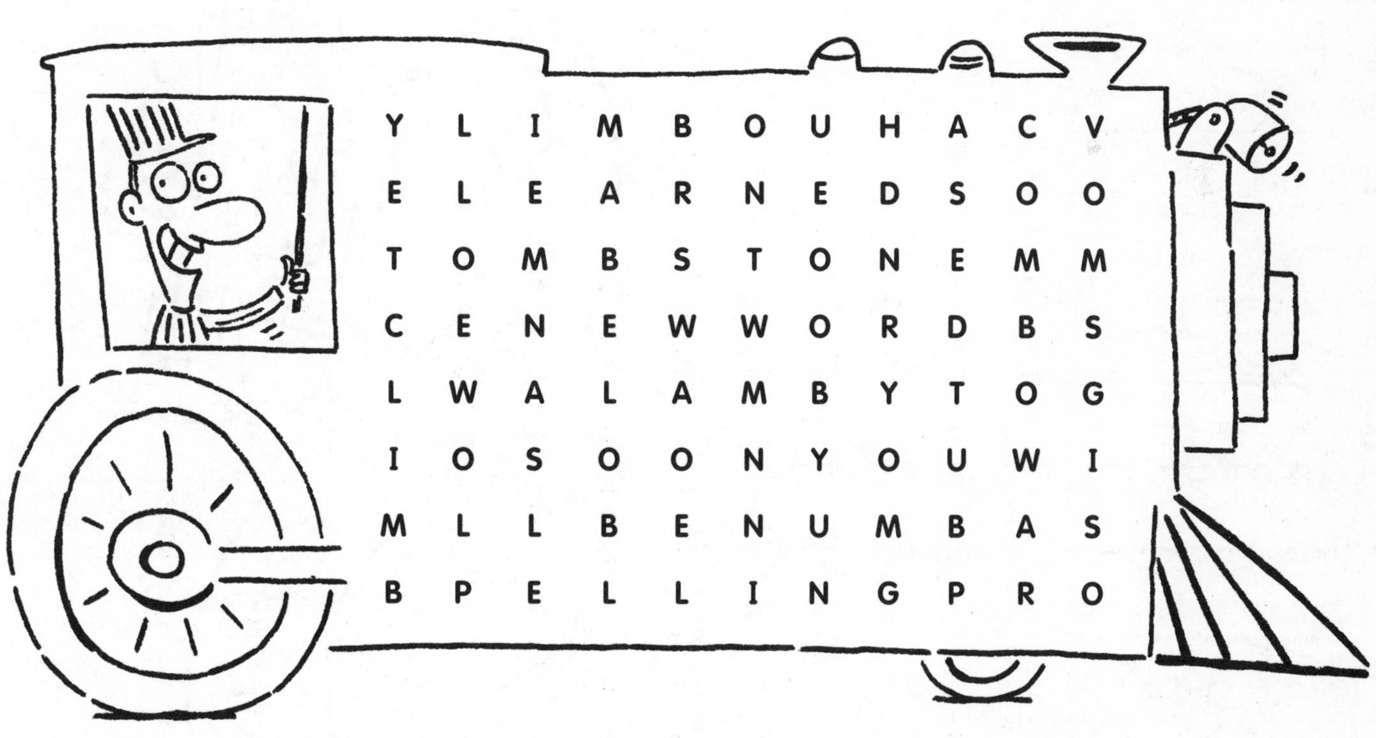

Now write all of the unused letters from the puzzle on the lines below. You will get this secret message:

_ _ _   _ _ _ _   _ _ _ _ _ _ _   _ _ _ _   _ _ _

_ _ _ _ _;   _ _ _   _ _   _ _!   _ _ _ _   _ _ _   _ _ _ _

_ _   _   _ _ _ _ _ _ _ _   _ _ _!

Spelling Secrets   Scholastic Professional Books

Name ______________________________

Date ______________________________

Alternate spellings of the /s/ sound

Spelling Snake

Spelling Secret

Most words use the letter *s* to make the /s/ sound. But some words use *c* or *sc* to make this sound.

This snake is made up of ten words that use the /s/ sound. Start at the bottom of the page. List the words you find on the lines below.

List the words:

____

____

____

____

____

____

____

____

____

____

STARCITYSNORESCISSORSSONCIRCLESCENESILLYSCIENTISTCIDER

Be a Super Speller!

On a separate sheet of paper put the words in ABC order. Then write a story using all ten of the words you found. Use your imagination!

Teaching Activities

Vowel Tic-Tac-Toe

Use with Kids' Pages 21–23.

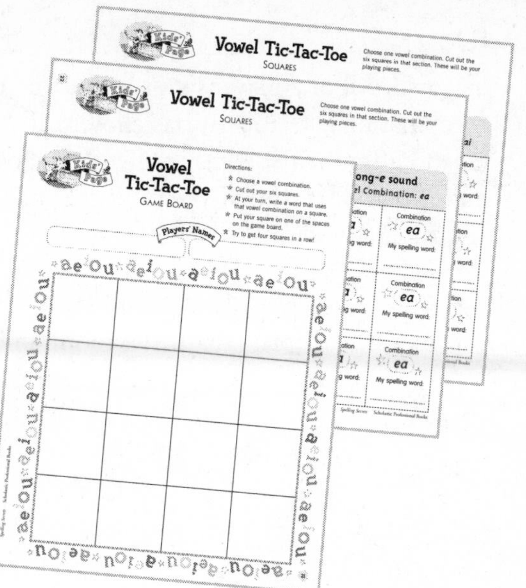

Here's a game to give students practice in spelling words that use unusual spellings for long-vowel sounds. The activity focuses on vowel combinations that make the long-*o*, -*a*, and -*e* sounds.

Alternate spellings of long-*o*, -*a*, and -*e* sounds

You Will Need

 copy of Kids' Page 21 (game board) for each pair of students

 copies of Kids' Pages 22–23 (vowel squares) for each pair of students

 scissors

- pencils
- double-sided tape (optional)

How to Play

1 Divide the class into pairs and provide each pair with a copy of the game board.

2 Decide which vowel combinations you would like to review. Assign each pair of students a vowel sound, and have each student choose one combination that spells that sound. For example, if a pair of students is playing with the long-*e* sound, one might choose the combination -*ea*, while the other uses the combination -*ie*. Give each student six squares for his or her combination. NOTE: You may have all student pairs work on the same vowel sound or have different teams work on different sounds.

3 Explain that this game is played just like regular Tic-Tac-Toe, except that players must get four in a row instead of three. Instead of using X's and O's, students will use their vowel squares. At each turn, they will write a word that uses their chosen vowel combination on a square, then place the square on the game board. To win, they must place four squares in a row. Rows may go across, down, or on the

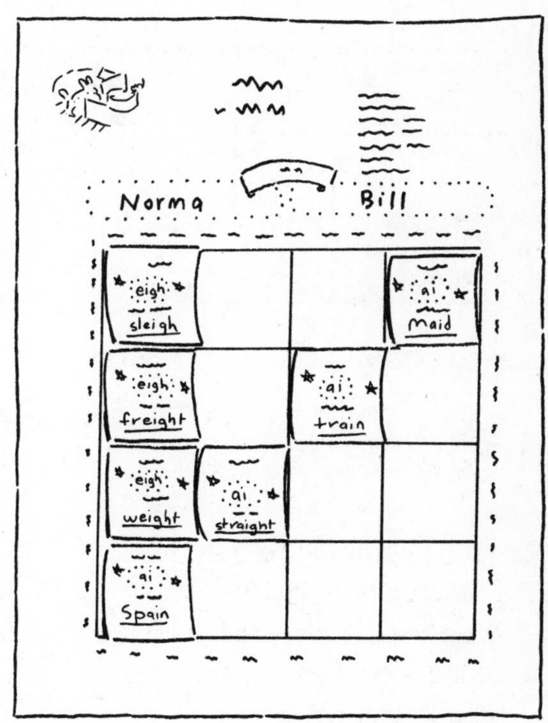

diagonal. All of a player's words must be correctly spelled and must use the vowel combination the student has chosen. If you'd like, have students use double-sided tape to affix their squares to the game board. That prevents squares from slipping out of place. (If students remove the tape carefully, you can reuse the game board and squares without making fresh photocopies. Or laminate the game boards and squares before use.)

4 As students play, roam the room and offer assistance as needed. Encourage students to consult a dictionary if they are unsure whether a word is spelled correctly.

When all student pairs have finished playing, make a master list of the words they have come up with. Use the words to write a silly poem or rap song. For example:

> **Some words use *ow* to spell *long o***
> **Like *know, slow, scarecrow, flow,* and *low.***
> **Others use *oa* to spell that sound,**
> **Like *toad, foam,* and *roam.* Examples abound!**

Point out that this game does not cover all possible ways to spell each vowel sound. For example, the long-*a* sound can be spelled with an *a* and a silent *e* as in *cane* and *dare.* It can also be spelled *ay* as in *hay* and *maybe.* Invite students to list at least one additional way to spell each vowel sound.

Vowel Tic-Tac-Toe

GAME BOARD

Directions:

- ★ Choose a vowel combination.
- ★ Cut out your six squares.
- ★ At your turn, write a word that uses that vowel combination on a square.
- ★ Put your square on one of the spaces on the game board.
- ★ Try to get four squares in a row!

Players' Names

Vowel Tic-Tac-Toe

SQUARES

Choose one vowel combination. Cut out the six squares in that section. These will be your playing pieces.

Long-*o* sound
Vowel Combination: ***ow***

Combination **ow** My spelling word: __________	Combination **ow** My spelling word: __________
Combination **ow** My spelling word: __________	Combination **ow** My spelling word: __________
Combination **ow** My spelling word: __________	Combination **ow** My spelling word: __________

Long-*o* sound
Vowel Combination: ***oa***

Combination **oa** My spelling word: __________	Combination **oa** My spelling word: __________
Combination **oa** My spelling word: __________	Combination **oa** My spelling word: __________
Combination **oa** My spelling word: __________	Combination **oa** My spelling word: __________

Long-*e* sound
Vowel Combination: ***ea***

Combination **ea** My spelling word: __________	Combination **ea** My spelling word: __________
Combination **ea** My spelling word: __________	Combination **ea** My spelling word: __________
Combination **ea** My spelling word: __________	Combination **ea** My spelling word: __________

Vowel Tic-Tac-Toe

SQUARES

Choose one vowel combination. Cut out the six squares in that section. These will be your playing pieces.

Long-*e* sound Vowel Combination: *ie*		Long-*a* sound Vowel Combination: *eigh*		Long-*a* sound Vowel Combination: *ai*	
Combination ☆ *ie* ☆ My spelling word: ____	Combination ☆ *ie* ☆ My spelling word: ____	Combination ☆ *eigh* ☆ My spelling word: ____	Combination ☆ *eigh* ☆ My spelling word: ____	Combination ☆ *ai* ☆ My spelling word: ____	Combination ☆ *ai* ☆ My spelling word: ____
Combination ☆ *ie* ☆ My spelling word: ____	Combination ☆ *ie* ☆ My spelling word: ____	Combination ☆ *eigh* ☆ My spelling word: ____	Combination ☆ *eigh* ☆ My spelling word: ____	Combination ☆ *ai* ☆ My spelling word: ____	Combination ☆ *ai* ☆ My spelling word: ____
Combination ☆ *ie* ☆ My spelling word: ____	Combination ☆ *ie* ☆ My spelling word: ____	Combination ☆ *eigh* ☆ My spelling word: ____	Combination ☆ *eigh* ☆ My spelling word: ____	Combination ☆ *ai* ☆ My spelling word: ____	Combination ☆ *ai* ☆ My spelling word: ____

Which One (Won) Is It?

(Homophones)

Students often have trouble with words that sound the same but have different meanings and spellings. Here, find tips and practice in choosing the right homophone.

One especially tricky area of English spelling is homophones, words that sound alike but have entirely different meanings and spellings. The word *homophone* comes from the Greek words *homo* (same) and *phonos* (sound). Because there are several other language arts terms with similar roots, you may find it helpful to distinguish *homophone* from these other words:

- **Homonyms:** The word *homonym* comes from the Greek words meaning "same" and "name." Homonyms are words that are spelled alike and sound alike, but have different meanings. An example is the word *pool*: I drive in a car *pool*, have a *pool* table at home, and swim in a *pool* on weekends.
- **Homographs:** These words are spelled the same but have different pronunciations or meanings. An example is the word *record*: I set a new *record* but I *record* a message on an answering machine.
- **Synonyms:** These are words that have the same meaning. They generally do not have the same spelling or sound.
- **Antonyms:** These are words that have opposite meanings.

Of course when it comes to spelling, homophones can be very confusing. Just when a student thinks he has a word's spelling down pat, he may encounter a new word that sounds exactly the same but has a different spelling. The activities in this section will help students master many of the most common homophones. Examples of frequently misused homophones include:

ant/aunt	**for/four**	**meet/meat**	**their/they're/there**
ate/eight	**hair/hare**	**one/won**	**threw/through**
bare/bear	**hear/here**	**piece/peace**	**to/two/too**
brake/break	**hour/our**	**right/write**	**wait/weight**
dear/deer	**know/no**	**steal/steel**	**wear/where**
flour/flower	**mail/male**	**tail/tale**	**witch/which**

Name ______________________

Date ______________________

Which Word?

Cut out the words on the right along the dotted lines. Paste each word in the sentence where it belongs.

Spelling Secret

Some words sound alike but have different spellings and meanings. They are called *homophones*.

1. The campers spotted a brown [ ] .
2. I need [ ] shoes.
3. Do you know [ ] my glasses are?
4. My neighbors left [ ] lights on.
5. I love walking in [ ] feet.
6. I hope there will be [ ] in the world.
7. Oliver wants to [ ] his new tie.
8. May I have a [ ] of cake?
9. Cecilia [ ] it was going to rain.
10. Whew! It was too hot in [ ] !

where
knew
wear
piece
peace
new
their
bare
bear
there

spelling homophones

Homophone Cupboard Mini-Book

Use with Kids' Pages 27–28.

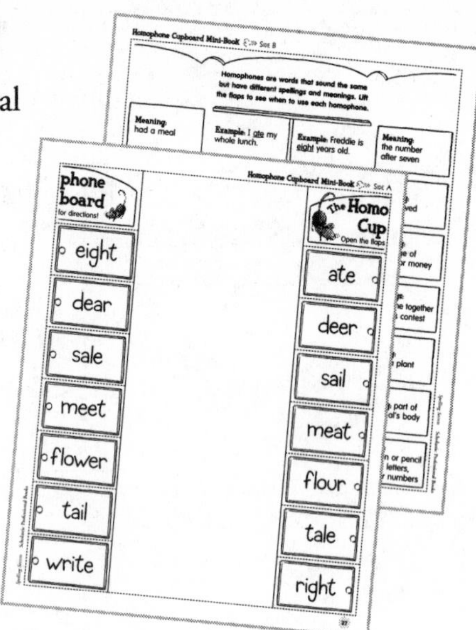

This make-it-yourself manipulative will help students remember how to use and spell several frequently used homophones. It is an excellent tool for quizzing oneself or a partner.

You Will Need

 double-sided copy of Kids' Pages 27-28 for each student

 scissors

 markers or crayons

What to Do

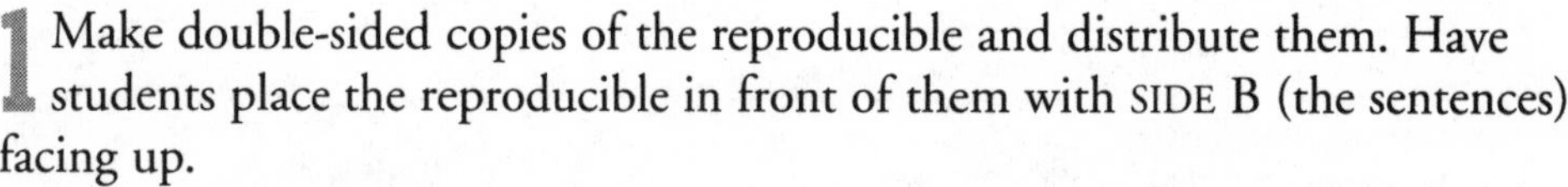

1 Make double-sided copies of the reproducible and distribute them. Have students place the reproducible in front of them with SIDE B (the sentences) facing up.

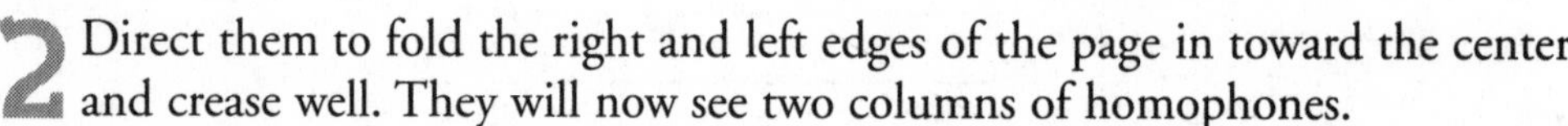

2 Direct them to fold the right and left edges of the page in toward the center and crease well. They will now see two columns of homophones.

3 Have students cut along the horizontal dotted lines to create sixteen doors or flaps.

4 Show students how to read the homophone on the front of each door and then open the door to check the word's usage. On the last pair of homophones (*right* and *write*), invite students to write their own sample sentences inside the doors.

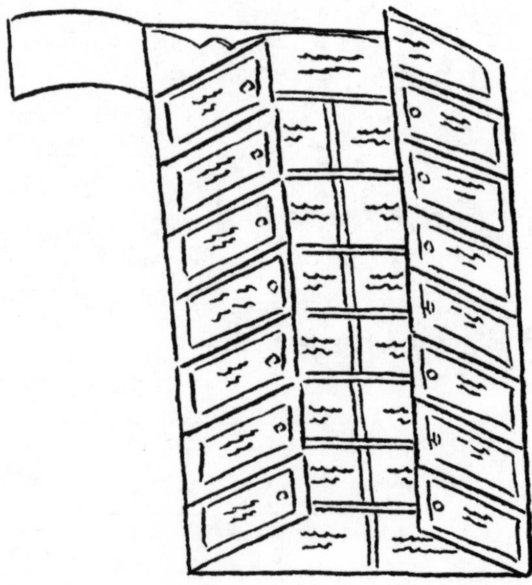

Using a plain sheet of paper, have students make similar "cupboards" for other homophones that are a challenge to remember.

eight	ate
dear	deer
sale	sail
meet	meat
flower	flour
tail	tale
write	right

Homophones are words that sound the same but have different spellings and meanings. Lift the flaps to see when to use each homophone.

Meaning: had a meal	**Example:** I ate my whole lunch.	**Example:** Freddie is eight years old.	**Meaning:** the number after seven
Meaning: a forest animal	**Example:** A deer and her fawn ran through the woods.	**Example:** Pam is a dear friend.	**Meaning:** much loved
Meaning: to travel by boat	**Example:** The ship will sail tomorrow.	**Example:** The school is having a bake sale.	**Meaning:** exchange of goods for money
Meaning: part of an animal used for food	**Example:** Beef and lamb are two kinds of meat.	**Example:** Let's meet at the track meet.	**Meanings:** 1. to come together 2. sports contest
Meaning: ground wheat used in baking	**Example:** He added flour to the cake batter.	**Example:** Jack gave his mom a flower for her birthday.	**Meaning:** part of a plant
Meaning: story	**Example:** Have you ever heard the tale of Sleeping Beauty?	**Example:** The puppy wagged its tail.	**Meaning:** part of an animal's body
Meanings: 1. correct 2. the opposite of left	Write your own sentence using right: ____ ____	Write your own sentence using write: ____ ____	**Meaning:** use a pen or pencil to record letters, words, or numbers

Spelling the homophones *their, they're,* and *there*

Name ______________________

Date ______________________

Their, They're, or There?

Spelling Secret

The word ***their*** is a possessive pronoun showing ownership: That's *their* car. The word ***they're*** is a contraction of "they are": ***They're*** visiting us today. The word ***there*** refers to a place: ***There*** is my hat!

Read each sentence and circle the correct homophone.

1. The Robinsons bought (*their, they're, there*) home two years ago.
2. Don't lock the car! My bag is still in (*their, they're, there*).
3. Ask your sisters if (*their, they're, there*) going to the carnival.
4. Oh no! (*Their, They're, There*) goes the school bus.
5. Dogs wag (*their, they're, there*) tails when (*their, they're, there*) happy.
6. (*Their, They're, There*) are more students in Room 3 than in Room 4.
7. I love Disney World. I have been (*their, they're, there*) two times.
8. The students can't wait to perform (*their, they're, there*) play.

Write a sentence using the word *their*.

____

Write a sentence using the word *they're*.

____

Write a sentence using the word *there*.

____

The To-Too-Two Square

Use with Kids' Pages 31–32.

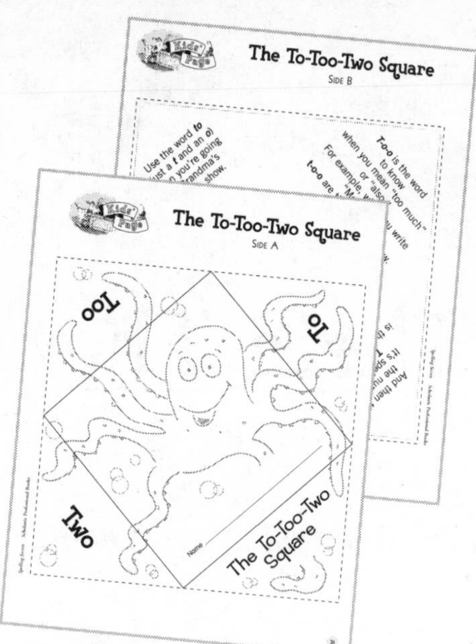

In this activity students construct manipulatives to help them remember when to use the homophones *to, too,* and *two.* After making the squares and enjoying the rhyme, have students show what they've learned by writing sentences using *to, too,* and *two.*

Spelling the homophones *to, too,* and *two*

You Will Need

 double-sided copy of Kids' Pages 31-32 for each student (Copy onto heavyweight paper for added durability.)

What to Do

1 Begin with a discussion of the words *to, too,* and *two*—some of the most commonly misused words in the English language. Write the words on the board, and ask students to give sentences using each one. Point out that it can be difficult to remember which spelling to use, and that students are going to make a rhyming tool to help them remember.

2 Have students put the reproducible on their desk with SIDE B facing up.

3 Direct them to fold in each of the four corners along the solid lines so that the points meet at the star in the center. They should now have a square with four triangular-shaped flaps on top.

4 Explain that students can open the flaps to read a rhyme about the words *to, too,* and *two.* Have them start with the title flap, then move in any direction (the stanzas can be read in any order). Read the rhyme together several times to help it stick in students' memories.

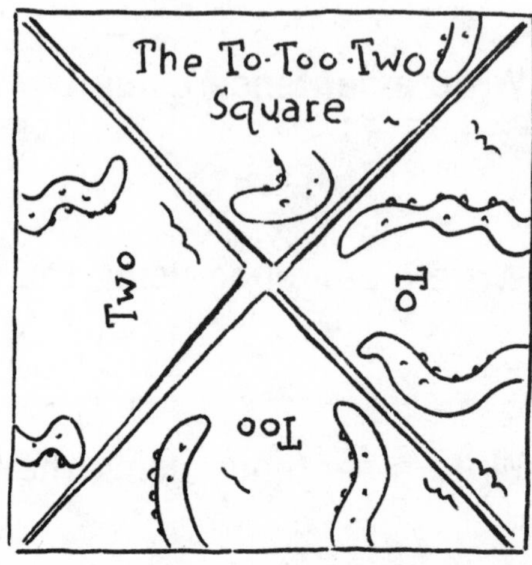

The To-Too-Two Square

SIDE A

Too

To

Two

Name

The To-Too-Two Square

The To-Too-Two Square

SIDE B

Use the word ***to***
(just a ***t*** and an ***o***)
when you're going
to Grandma's
or ***to*** a show.

T-o-o is the word
to know
when you mean "too much"
or "also."
For example, when you write
"Me, ***too***,"
t-o-o are the letters to show.

★

There are three
little words
that all sound like ***to***.
Are you mixed up?
This rhyme will help you!

And then there is
the number ***two***.
It's spelled with a ***w***!
T-w-o, you see,
is the number that comes
before three.

Putting Words Together

(Compound Words and Contractions)

Sometimes even the best spellers have problems combining words to make other words. Help students brush up on compound words and contractions.

As you begin this section, point out to students that a *compound word* is two or more smaller words put together to make a single word. A *contraction* is a word formed by putting together two words with certain letters left out. An apostrophe is used in place of the missing letters. Many young writers struggle with the spellings of both compound words and contractions. They may write a compound word as two or more separate words instead of a single word. They may also forget or misplace the apostrophe in a contraction.

In this chapter your students get practice writing and spelling frequently used compound words and contractions. For your convenience, lists of both types of words follow:

Some Commonly Used Compound Words

anteater
backpack
baseball
bookcase
cupcake
daydream
daytime
dishwasher
eggshell
eyeball
fingernail
firefighter
footprint
homework
keyboard
lighthouse
railroad
seashell
snowball
sunshine
teardrop
toolbox
toothpaste
touchdown

Some Commonly Used Contractions

aren't	are not
can't	cannot
couldn't	could not
could've	could have
didn't	did not
doesn't	does not
don't	do not
hadn't	had not
hasn't	has not
haven't	have not
he'd	he would/he had
he'll	he will
he's	he is
I'm	I am
isn't	is not
it'll	it will
it's	it is
let's	let us
she'd	she would/she had
she'll	she will
she's	she is
shouldn't	should not
should've	should have

there's	there is
they'll	they will
they're	they are
wasn't	was not
we'll	we will
we're	we are
weren't	were not
what's	what is
won't	will not
wouldn't	would not
would've	would have
you'll	you will
you're	you are

Spelling compound words

Name ______________________

Date ______________________

Build-a-Word Crossword Puzzle

Spelling Secret

A compound word is made up of two or more smaller words.

Find the compound word that completes each sentence by putting together two small words from the Word Box. Each word from the Word Box can be used only once. Write your answers in the crossword puzzle.

Word Box

star	door	base
tool	paste	cake
bell	sun	box
rain	head	finger
ball	ache	print
cup	fish	tooth
burn	drop	

Crossword Clues

ACROSS

2. For dessert, I ate a chocolate _______ .
6. The police found the thief's _______ on the stolen bag.
8. I can't brush my teeth because I'm out of _______ .
9. The Yankees are my favorite _______ team.
10. When I heard the _______ ring, I knew my guests had arrived.

DOWN

1. Nadia opened her umbrella after she felt a _______ on her head.
3. A _______ is a sea creature with five legs.
4. Benjamin got a painful _______ at the beach.
5. The loud music gave Oliver a _______ .
7. Dad keeps the hammer in his _______ .

Kids' Page

Name ______________________

Date ______________________

Focus

Spelling compound words

Spelling Secret

If you can spell the small words that make up a compound word, you can spell the compound word!

Make a compound-word garden! Cut out the flower centers, petals, and leaves on this page and page 37. Read the word inside each flower center. On a separate sheet of paper, glue the four flower centers, leaving space between them. Then paste four petals around each flower center to make four compound words. Draw a stem on your flower and paste a leaf to it. Write the compound words on the lines on the leaf.

Flower Power

PART 1

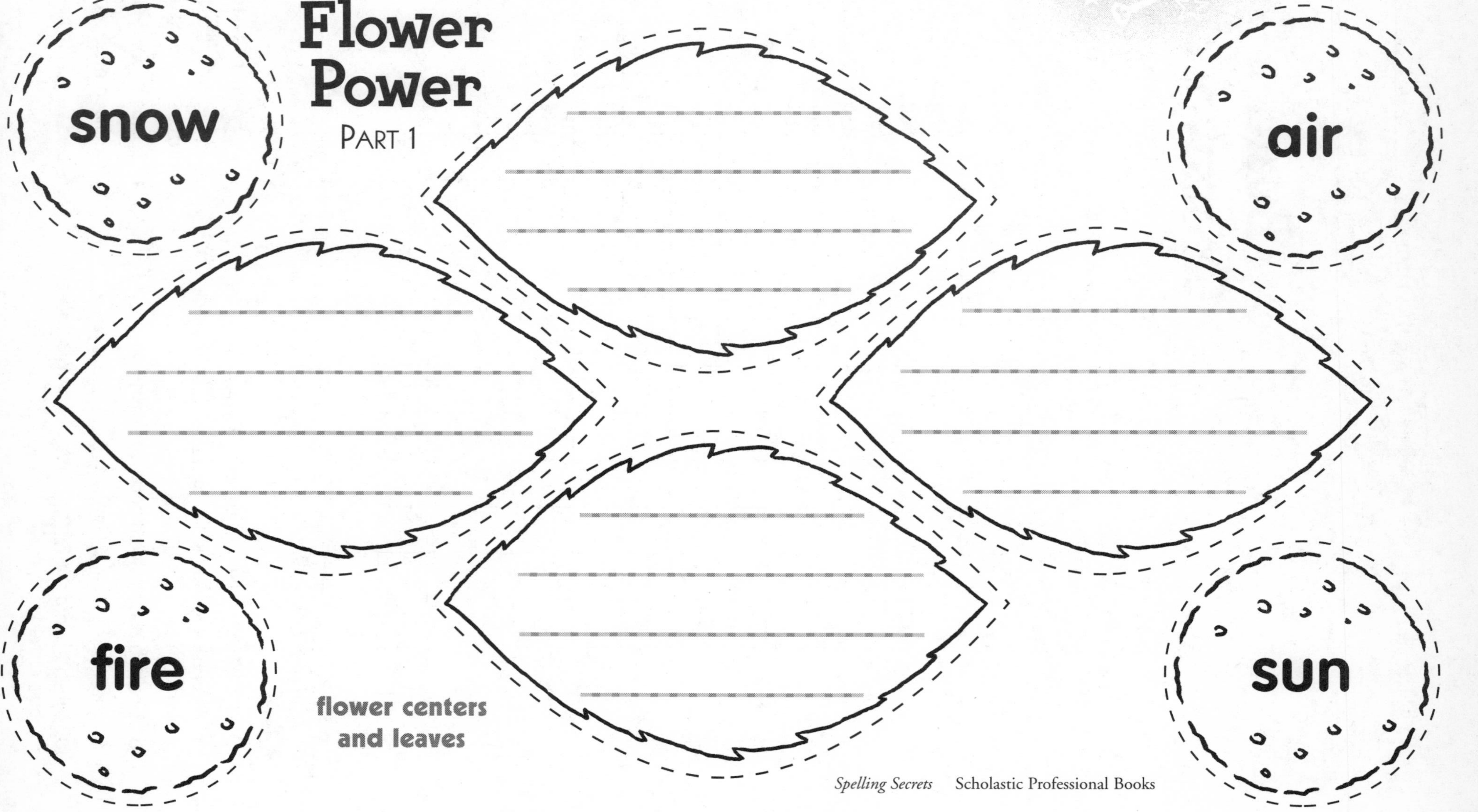

flower centers and leaves

Flower Power
Part 2

flower petals

fighter

ball

burn

day

mail

line

fly

flake

mobile

place

plane

port

set

shine

storm

works

Spelling contractions

Contraction Action Card Game

Use with Kids' Pages 39–40.

Here's a Concentration-style card game that will help students remember which words can be combined to form contractions, which letters are left out, and where the apostrophe goes. Students can play in groups of two or three. The game is simple to prepare and play.

You Will Need

- copy of Kids' Page 39 (one My Word List for each student)
- copy of Kids' Page 40 for each group of students
- scissors
-  dictionaries

What to Do

1 Make copies of the reproducible cards (page 40) for each group. Have students cut along the lines to separate the 30 cards. Also distribute one My Word List (page 39) to each student.

2 Demonstrate how to play: The first player should turn over two cards. If they can be joined together to form a contraction, the player should keep the cards in his or her pile and write the contraction on his or her word list. Students should have access to a dictionary to check their spellings. The next player can then take a turn.

3 The game ends when all cards have been used or when both players agree that the remaining cards do not form a contraction. (Note that because the words can be combined in various ways to form contractions, players may have two or four leftover cards. For example, the word *I* can be combined with *will*, *have*, *am*, and *would*. Because of this flexibility, it is possible to form pairs in such a way that the final remaining cards do not go together.) The player with the most contractions on his or her list is the winner.

Concentration Action

My Word List

Name ____________________

My Word List

Name ____________________

My Word List

Name ____________________

am	he	is	not	will
are	he	it	she	will
are	I	let	they	would
do	I	not	us	would
have	is	not	was	you
have	is	not	we	you

Name ______________________________

Date ______________________________

Calling All Contractions!

Rewrite each sentence, replacing the underlined phrase with a contraction. On the line at the end of the sentence, write the letter or letters you took out to form the contraction.

Spelling Secret

In a contraction, the apostrophe takes the place of the missing letter or letters.

1. Let us share some popcorn.

   ______________________________ ________

2. I am a Girl Scout.

   ______________________________ ________

3. We will see you tomorrow.

   ______________________________ ________

4. I do not have a pencil.

   ______________________________ ________

5. She is my best friend.

   ______________________________ ________

6. He would like a hamburger.

   ______________________________ ________

7. Olivia should have taken the bus.

   ______________________________ ________

8. What is your favorite movie?

   ______________________________ ________

9. They are planning a party.

   ______________________________ ________

10. We could not find the path.

    ______________________________ ________

Now use the missing letters from some of the sentences to finish the answer to this riddle. The numbers stand for the sentences.

Why did the bird fly south for the winter?

S___ ___t
(10) (5)

___ ___ ___ ___d
(6)

n___t h___ve
(4) (9)

t___ w___ ___t
(10) (9) (8)

f___r the b___s!
(4) (1)

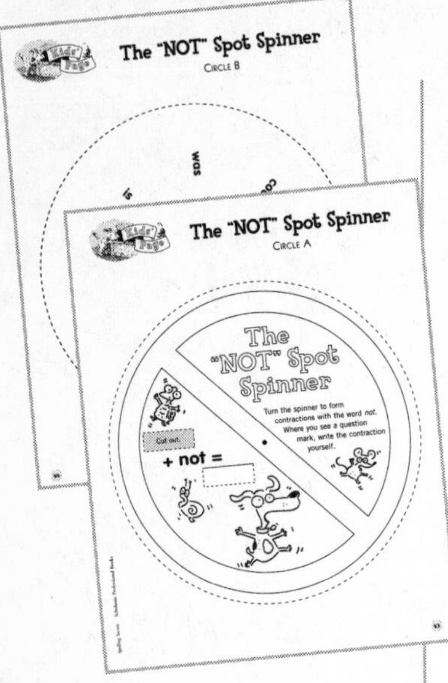

Spelling contractions

The "NOT" Spot Spinner Game

Use with Kids' Pages 43–44.

Many of the contractions we use frequently incorporate the word *not.* You can probably name several examples off the top of your head, including *can't, won't, don't, shouldn't, wouldn't, couldn't, isn't, aren't, hasn't, haven't.* The challenge for many students in spelling contractions with the word *not* is remembering where to place the apostrophe. Many young writers are tempted to place the punctuation between the two words that are being joined. For example, they may write *is'nt* instead of *isn't* or *do'nt* instead of *don't.* The trick is to remember that the apostrophe goes wherever the letters have been taken out—not necessarily between the two words. One example to highlight is the contraction *won't,* which is formed from the words *will not.* Here, letters are removed in two spots to form the contraction (the *-ill* and the *o* are removed and an *o* is added just after the *w*). You might suggest that students memorize this confusing contraction!

In this activity students construct a spinner that will quiz them on and remind them of the spelling of eight frequently used "not" contractions. Have students hang on to their spinners for ongoing reference!

You Will Need

- copies of Kids' Pages 43–44 for each student
- scissors
- brass fasteners
- pens or pencils

What to Do

1 Have students cut out the two circles. On CIRCLE A, help students cut along the dotted lines to create two rectangular windows. The bottom window will have a flap attached.

2 Direct students to put CIRCLE A on top of CIRCLE B. Then they secure a brass fastener through the center of the two circles.

3 Have students rotate the spinners until "do" appears in the top window. Point out the word equation on the spinner ("do" + "not" =) and show students how to lift the flap to reveal the proper spelling of the contraction "don't."

4 Students can continue to rotate the spinners, lifting the flap to check the spelling of each of the first four contractions. For the last four examples, a blank space with a question mark has been provided under the flap. For these, students should fill in the correct spelling of the contraction that is formed.

The "NOT" Spot Spinner

CIRCLE A

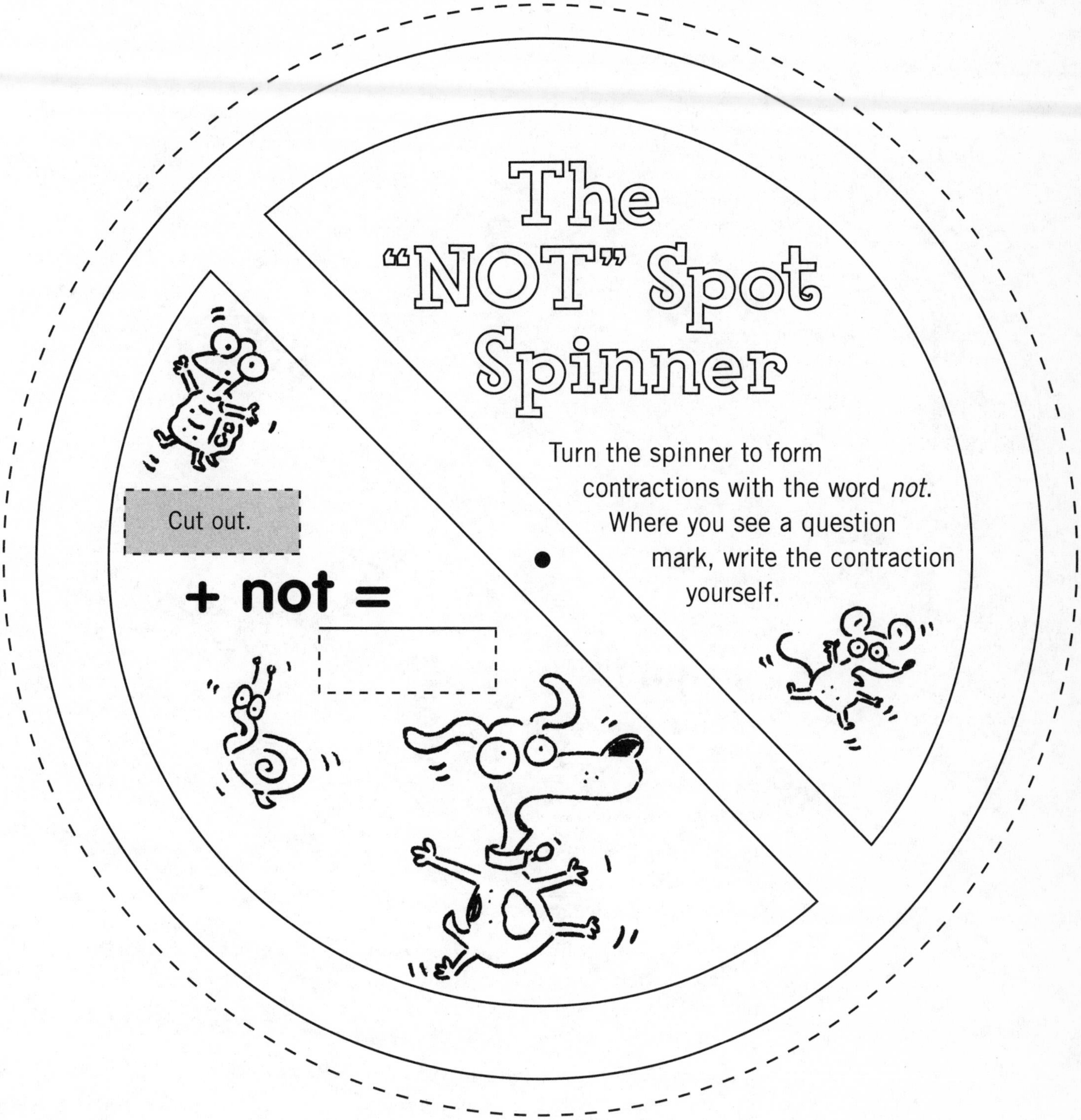

The "NOT" Spot Spinner

Turn the spinner to form contractions with the word *not*. Where you see a question mark, write the contraction yourself.

Cut out.

+ not =

Kids' Page

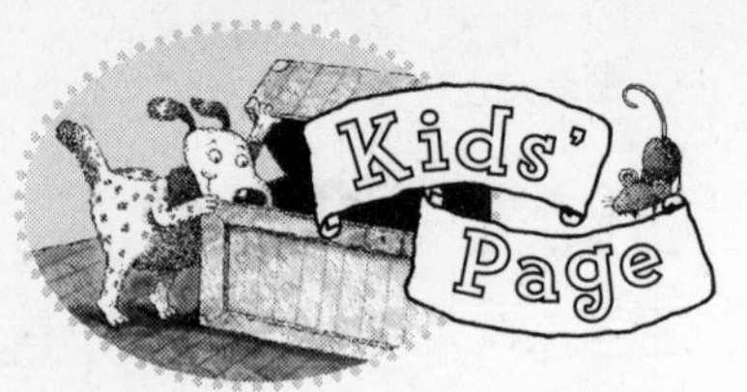

The "NOT" Spot Spinner

CIRCLE B

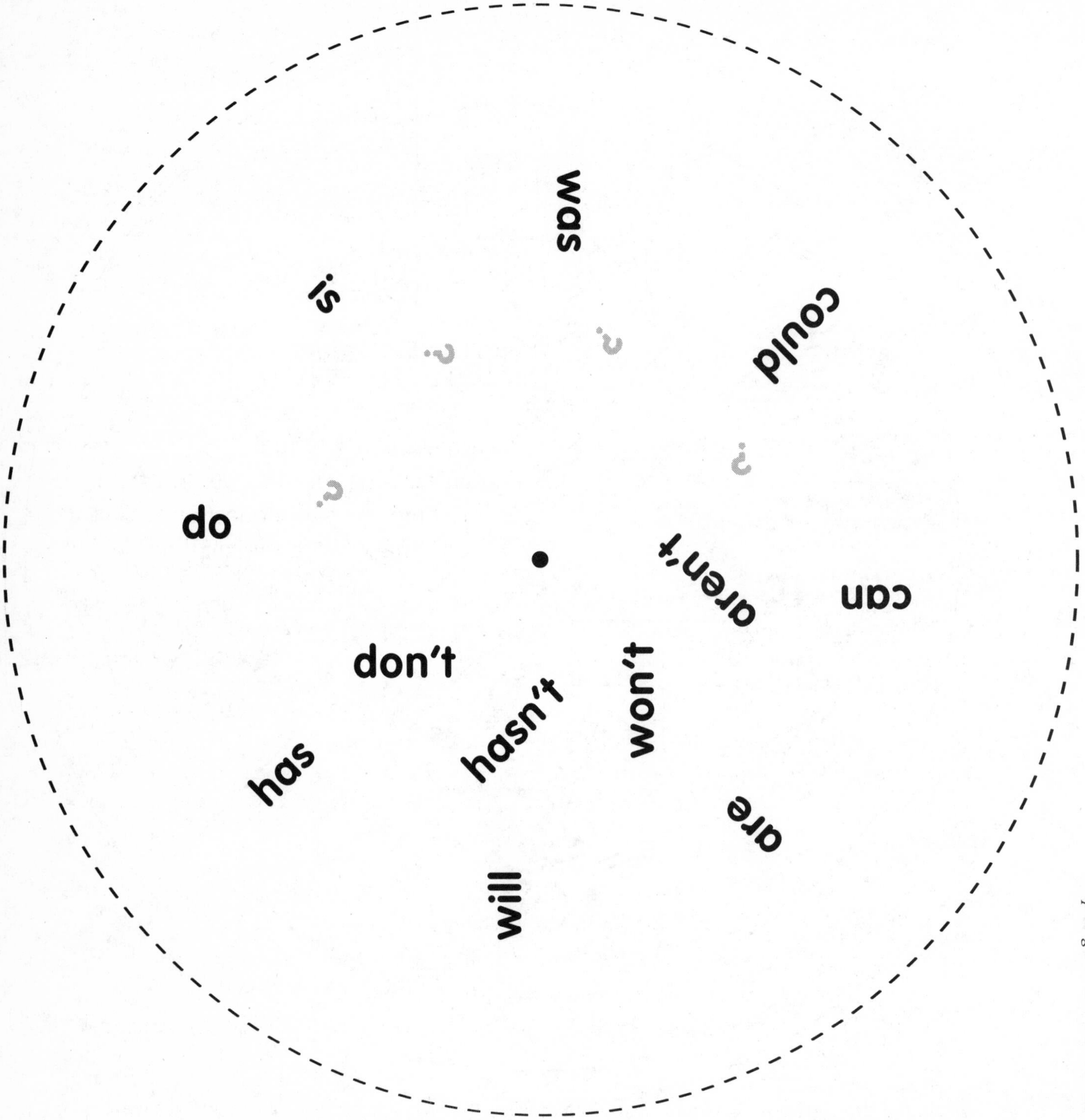
was
is
could
?
?
?
?
do
aren't
can
don't
won't
hasn't
has
are
will

Rules Rule!

(Plurals and Past-Tense Verbs)

Some spelling rules can be applied to large numbers of words. For example, we add -s or -es to form the plural of many nouns and add -ed to form the past tense of verbs. In this chapter, students get to know the basic rules and a few exceptions.

Do you have students who have no trouble spelling simple words like *watch* and *call*, but make spelling errors when they try to put the words in plural form or past tense (they may write *watchs* and *calld* instead of *watches* and *called*)? Or do you have kids who consistently put the *e* before the *i* in words such as *piece* or *believe*? These types of spelling errors are not uncommon among second-, third-, and fourth-graders, who are beginning to write more sophisticated stories and essays. Their vocabularies are growing in leaps and bounds, but their spelling skills may lag behind a bit.

The good news for young spellers is that there are some easy-to-remember rules that can help them tackle many of the words they want to write. In this chapter, you'll find activities to help students learn and remember spelling rules that can be applied to large numbers of words. Many of these rules come into play when making a structural change to a word students already know how to spell. These rules include:

- Forming the plural of a noun by adding *-s*, *-es*, or changing the *-y* to an *i* and adding *-es*.
- Forming the past tense of a regular verb by adding *-ed*.
- Putting *i* before e except after *c* or when sounding like *ay*, as in *neighbor* or *weigh*.
- Dropping a silent *e* when adding the suffix *-ing* to a word.
- Doubling the final consonant when adding suffixes to one-syllable words such as *nut* and *tan* (*nutty*, *tanned*).

Although there are a few exceptions to these rules (it *is* English, after all!), learning these basic patterns will give students a firm foundation in spelling.

Spelling plural nouns

Sammy's Eight Days of Camping Plurals Mini-Book

Use with Kids' Pages 47–49.

In this make-it-yourself mini-book, students get acquainted with the basic rules for spelling plural nouns and try their hand at spelling a word that follows each rule. Because the story builds in a cumulative pattern, students will write each plural noun several times—giving them plenty of important practice! Once students have finished making and using the manipulatives in class, have them share the mini-books with their families.

You Will Need

- copies of Kids' Pages 47-49 for each student
- pencils or pens
- markers or crayons
- stapler

What to Do

1. Have students cut out each page of the flip book (each is a different size) and compile the pages in numerical order.

2. Direct them to staple along the top edge to bind the book.

3. Invite students to read the mini-books, stopping to write the plural of each given noun on the blanks. Students can use the spelling hints on each page to form the plurals.

4. If you'd like, have students write additional examples of each pluralization rule on the reverse side of the page.

Sammy's Eight Days of Camping Plurals Mini-Book

Inside the book, fill in each blank with the plural form of the given noun. Use the spelling hints at the bottom of each page!

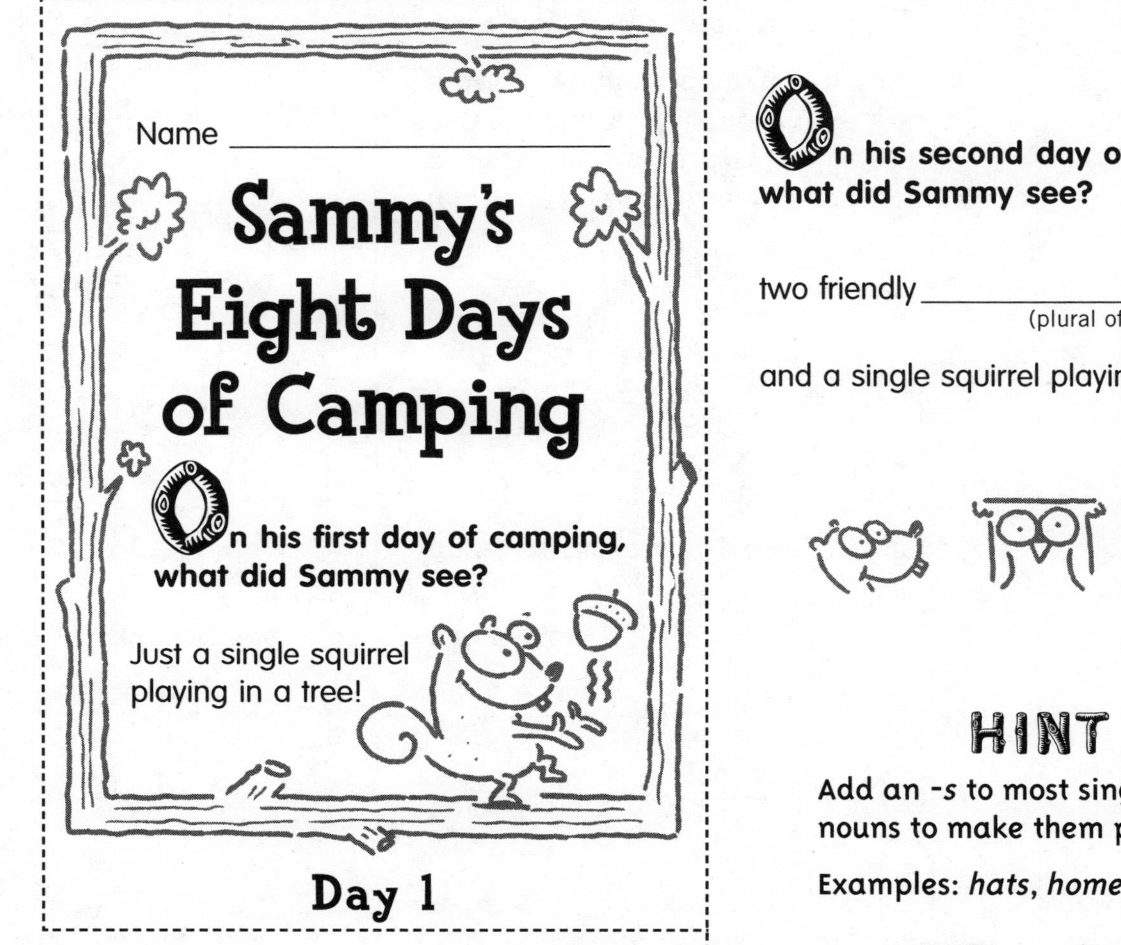

Name ______________________

Sammy's Eight Days of Camping

On his first day of camping, what did Sammy see?

Just a single squirrel playing in a tree!

Day 1

On his second day of camping, what did Sammy see?

two friendly ______________________ ,
(plural of *owl*)

and a single squirrel playing in a tree.

HINT

Add an *-s* to most singular nouns to make them plural.

Examples: *hats, homes*

Day 2

On his third day of camping, what did Sammy see?

three sneaky ________________, (plural of *fox*)

two friendly ________________, (plural of *owl*)

and a single squirrel playing in a tree.

HINT

If a noun ends in -*ch*, -*sh*, -*s*, -*x*, or -*z*, add -*es* to make it plural.

Examples: *churches*, *boxes*

Day 3

On his fourth day of camping, what did Sammy see?

four colorful ________________, (plural of *leaf*)

three sneaky ________________, (plural of *fox*)

two friendly ________________, (plural of *owl*)

and a single squirrel playing in a tree.

HINT

If a noun ends in -*f*, or -*lf*, you usually change the *f* to a *v* and add -*es* to make it plural. If it ends in -*fe*, you usually change the *f* to a *v* and add -*s*.

Examples: *wolves*, *knives*

Day 4

On his fifth day of camping, what did Sammy see?

five bouncing ________________, (plural of *bunny*)

four colorful ________________, (plural of *leaf*)

three sneaky ________________, (plural of *fox*)

two friendly ________________, (plural of *owl*)

and a single squirrel playing in a tree.

HINT

If a noun ends in a consonant followed by -*y*, drop the -*y* and add -*ies* to make it plural.

Examples: *flies*, *pennies*

Day 5

Sammy's Eight Days of Camping Plurals Mini-Book

On his sixth day of camping, what did Sammy see?

six swinging ______________ ,
(plural of *monkey*)

five bouncing ______________ ,
(plural of *bunny*)

four colorful ______________ ,
(plural of *leaf*)

three sneaky ______________ ,
(plural of *fox*)

two friendly ______________ ,
(plural of *owl*)

and a single squirrel playing in a tree.

HINT

If a noun ends in a vowel followed by -*y*, just add -*s* to make it plural.

Examples: *days*, *boys*

Day 6

On his seventh day of camping, what did Sammy see?

seven bright ______________ ,
(plural of *flamingo*)

six swinging ______________ ,
(plural of *monkey*)

five bouncing ______________ ,
(plural of *bunny*)

four colorful ______________ ,
(plural of *leaf*)

three sneaky ______________ ,
(plural of *fox*)

two friendly ______________ ,
(plural of *owl*)

and a single squirrel playing in a tree.

HINT

If a noun ends in a consonant followed by -*o*, add -*es* to make it plural.

Examples: *potatoes*, *heroes*

Day 7

On his eighth day of camping, what did Sammy see?

Eight merry ______________ ,
(plural of *mouse*)

seven bright ______________ ,
(plural of *flamingo*)

six swinging ______________ ,
(plural of *monkey*)

five bouncing ______________ ,
(plural of *bunny*)

four colorful ______________ ,
(plural of *leaf*)

three sneaky ______________ ,
(plural of *fox*)

two friendly ______________ ,
(plural of *owl*)

and a single squirrel playing in a tree.

WHEW!

HINT

Some nouns, like *mouse*, form odd plurals. Memorize them!

Examples: *children*, *feet*

Day 8

Sammy's Eight Days of Camping Plurals Mini-Book

Name ______________________ Date ______________

Focus
Spelling plural nouns

Crack the Plurals Code!

Two centuries ago the Morse code was used to send messages over electric wires. This code uses a combination of dots and dashes to stand for each letter of the alphabet. Use the Morse code to find the correct way to spell the plural form of each noun.

Spelling Secret

To form the plural of some nouns add *-s* or *-es*. For other nouns, drop the *-y* and add *-ies* to form the plural. Still other nouns are irregular and therefore form unusual plurals.

Noun	Crack the Code!	Write the Plural Form
TREE	– •–• • • •••	
GOOSE	––• • • ••• •	
WISH	•–– •• ••• •••• • •••	
SKI	••• –•– •• •••	
DIARY	–•• •• •– •–• •• • •••	
FOOT	••–• • • –	
FRIEND	••–• •–• •• • –• –•• •••	
BOX	–••• ––– –••– • •••	
DEER	–•• • • •–•	
KEY	–•– • –•–– •••	
SEA	••• • •– •••	
WOMAN	•–– ––– –– • –•	

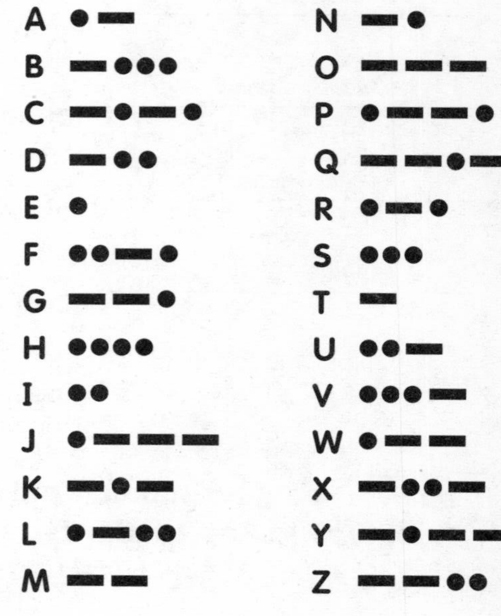

Morse Code

A	•–	N	–•
B	–•••	O	–––
C	–•–•	P	•––•
D	–••	Q	––•–
E	•	R	•–•
F	••–•	S	•••
G	––•	T	–
H	••••	U	••–
I	••	V	•••–
J	•–––	W	•––
K	–•–	X	–••–
L	•–••	Y	–•––
M	––	Z	––••

Name ______________________

Date ______________________

Focus
Adding *-ed* to form the past tense

Spelling Secret
Many verbs add the letters *-ed* to form the past tense. If the verb already ends in *-e*, just add *-d*.

Spell-the-Past-Tense-Perfectly! Word Search

Look at the underlined verb in each sentence. Use the spelling secret to rewrite it in the past tense. Then circle each past-tense verb in the puzzle. Words can go across, down, or on the diagonal.

1. We walk to school. ______________
2. I call my aunt. ______________
3. They open the mail. ______________
4. Squirrels gather nuts in our yard. ______________
5. We use too much electricity. ______________
6. Boats sail on the river. ______________
7. I print a page from the computer. ______________
8. We shovel snow for our neighbor. ______________
9. They miss their old home. ______________
10. I decide what to wear in the morning. ______________

G	O	N	S	D	E	C	I	D	E	D	T
A	H	W	A	L	K	E	D	E	P	D	P
T	A	G	I	E	S	U	O	F	E	M	R
H	W	E	L	B	S	T	S	L	E	I	I
E	O	P	E	N	E	D	L	E	R	S	N
R	S	D	D	I	C	A	T	I	D	S	T
E	O	N	A	R	C	Y	S	I	L	E	E
D	L	Y	S	H	O	V	E	L	E	D	D

Now write all of the unused letters from the puzzle on the lines below. They will spell the answer to this riddle!

Where in the world does Monday come before Sunday?

_ _ _ _ _ _ _ _ _ _ _ _ _ _

_ _ _ _ _ _ _ _ ' _ _ _ _ _ _ _ _ _ _ _ ,

_ _ _ _ _ _ !

Spelling past-tense verbs

Greetings From Camp Spelli-Melli! Past-Tense Slider

Use with Kids' Pages 54–55.

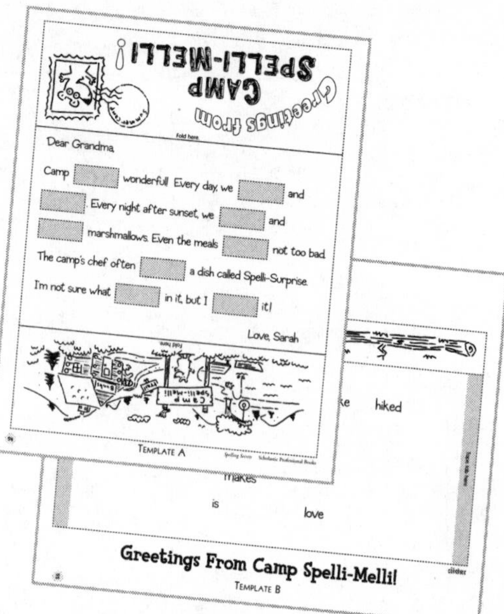

Oh no! Poor Sarah wrote her grandmother a postcard from summer camp—but she forgot to mail it! Now she must edit the postcard so that all the summer fun is in the past tense. Your students will have a blast making and using this past-tense slider. They can read the postcard in the present tense, then pull the slider to the right to put it in the past tense. They'll encounter both regular and irregular verbs: *is/was, hike/hiked, swim/swam, sing/sang, toast/toasted, are/were, makes/made, love/loved.* The first two verbs have been spelled for students, but it's up to them to fill in the rest.

You Will Need

- copies of Kids' Pages 54-55 for each student
- pencils or pens
- markers or crayons
- scissors
- tape or glue

What to Do

1 If possible, enlarge the templates when you photocopy them. Have students cut out the postcard (TEMPLATE A) along the outer dotted lines and color the illustrations around the border.

2 Direct students to cut out the windows on the postcard. (To do this, show students how to fold the postcard at a right angle to the dotted lines. Then they snip along the lines from the crease of the fold inward.)

3 Have students fold the postcard template along the solid lines. Then they tape together the two halves of the illustrated side of the postcard, creating an open sleeve.

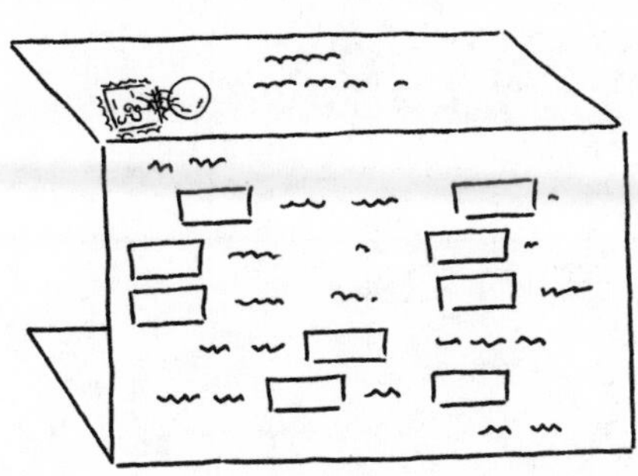

4 Now have students cut out the slider (TEMPLATE B) along the dotted lines.

5 Direct students to slip the slider into the folded postcard sleeve. To make sure the slider does not fall out, have them cut out the two rectangular "log" tabs from page 55 and tape or glue these to both ends of the slider.

6 Tell students to adjust the slider so that the verbs *is, hike, swim, sing, toast, are, makes, is,* and *love* are visible through the windows.

7 To transform the present-tense verbs into the past tense, they pull the slider to the left. The first two verbs have already been completed, so students will see the past-tense verbs *was* and *hiked* in the top two windows. Invite students to write the remaining past-tense verbs in the appropriate blank windows.

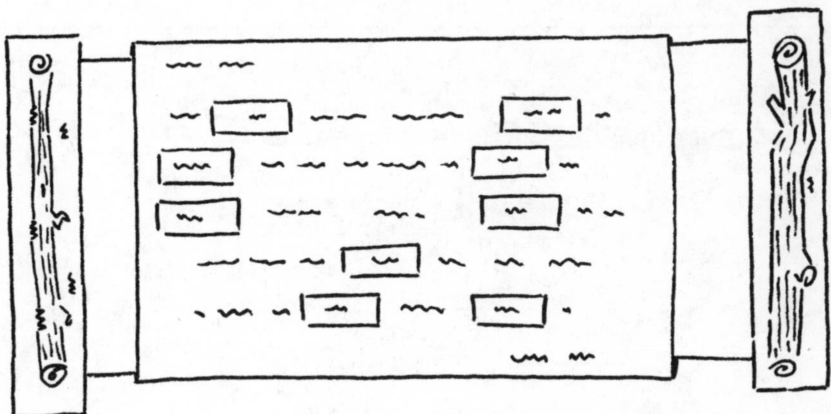

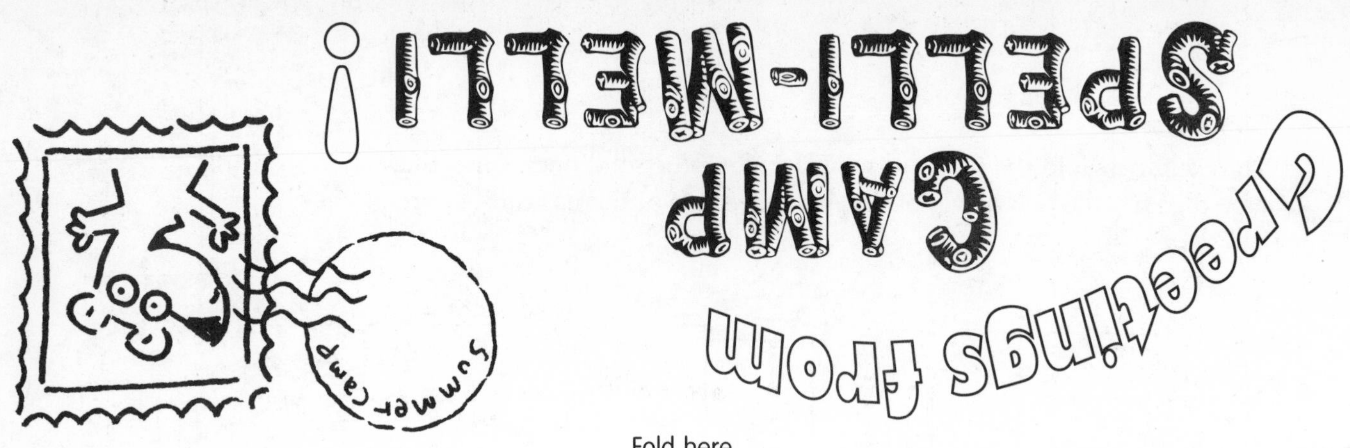

Fold here.

Dear Grandma,

Camp [ ] wonderful! Every day, we [ ] and [ ]. Every night after sunset, we [ ] and [ ] marshmallows. Even the meals [ ] not too bad. The camp's chef often [ ] a dish called Spelli-Surprise. I'm not sure what [ ] in it, but I [ ] it!

Love, Sarah

Fold here.

TEMPLATE A

tabs

Tape tab here.

is was hike hiked

swim sing

toast are

makes

is love

Tape tab here.

slider

Greetings From Camp Spelli-Melli! Past-Tense Slider

TEMPLATE B

Putting *i* before *e*

I Before E Mini-Book

Use with Kids' Pages 57–58.

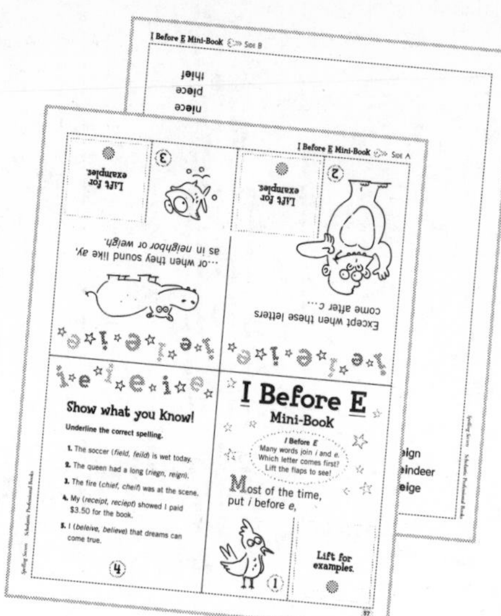

Finally, here is a fun way to teach that pesky but helpful spelling rule, "*I* before *E* except after *C*"! In this activity students construct a mini-book that outlines the "*I* before *E*" rule and offers plenty of examples. On the last page of the mini-book, kids apply what they have learned by taking a quick quiz.

You Will Need

-  double-sided copy of Kids' Pages 57-58 for each student
-  scissors
- markers or crayons

What to Do

1 Have students cut out the template along the dotted lines and place the page in front of them with SIDE A facing up.

2 Next they fold the top half of the page down along the solid horizontal line and crease well.

3 Then they fold the page in half again along the solid vertical line and crease well.

4 On pages 1, 2, and 3, direct them to cut along the vertical dotted lines at the bottom of each page.

5 Have students color the mini-books. Then read them together. Demonstrate how to lift the flap at the bottom of each page for examples of each aspect of the "*I* before *E*" rule.

6 Finally, have students tackle the "*I* before *E*" quiz on page 4 of the mini-book. Check answers and discuss any problem words.

Teacher's Note

Keep in mind that there are a few exceptions to the "*I* before *E*" rule. They include: *either*, *foreign*, *height*, *leisure*, *neither*, and *weird*.

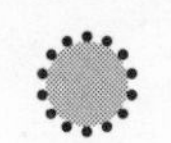

Lift for examples.

3

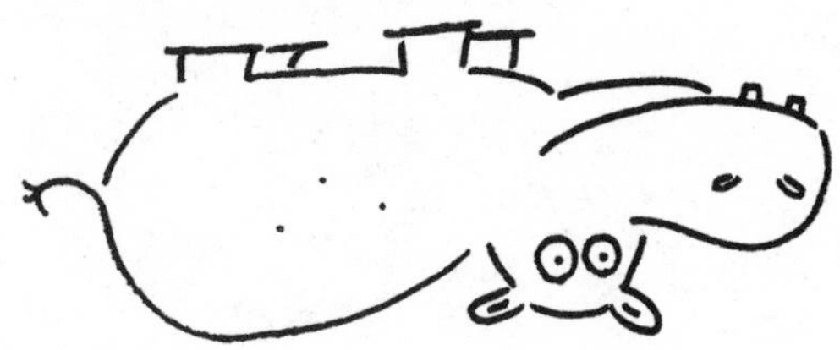

...or when they sound like *ay*,
as in *neighbor* or *weigh*.

Lift for examples.

2

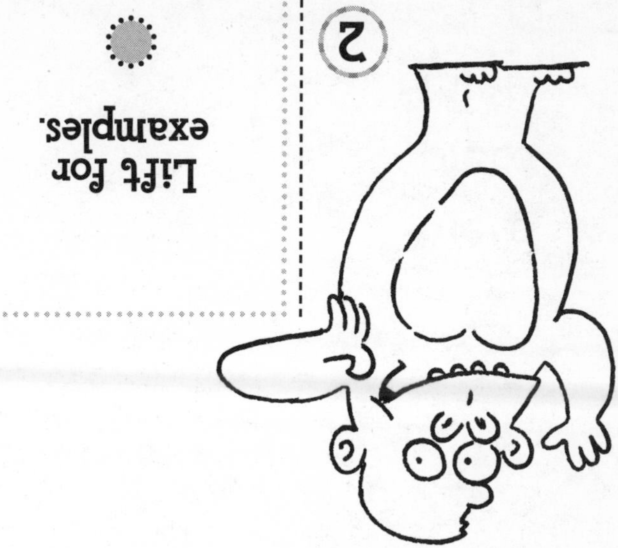

Except when these letters
come after *c*...

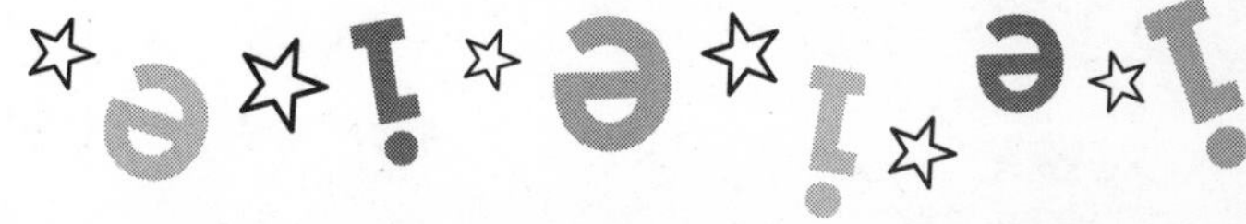

Show what you know!

Underline the correct spelling.

1. The soccer (*field*, *feild*) is wet today.
2. The queen had a long (*riegn*, *reign*).
3. The fire (*chief*, *cheif*) was at the scene.
4. My (*receipt*, *reciept*) showed I paid $3.50 for the book.
5. I (*beleive*, *believe*) that dreams can come true.

4

I Before E
Mini-Book

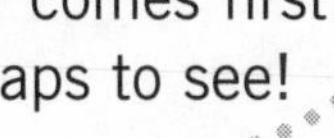

I* Before *E
Many words join *i* and *e*.
Which letter comes first?
Lift the flaps to see!

Most of the time,
put *i* before *e*,

1

Lift for examples.

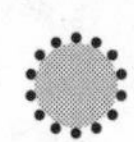

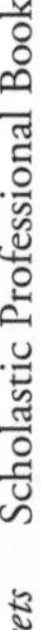

niece
piece
thief

c**ei**ling
dec**ei**ve
rec**ei**ve

r**ei**gn
r**ei**ndeer
b**ei**ge

Doubling a consonant or dropping a silent *e* when adding *-ing*

Name ______________________________

Date ______________________________

Presto Change-o! With -ing

To make words like *walking* and *smiling*, you need to add the letters *-ing* to a verb. To spell these words correctly, there are two secrets you should know! Check out the secrets, then try spelling the words that follow.

run + ing = ______________________

stir + ing = ______________________

set + ing = ______________________

put + ing = ______________________

sled + ing = ______________________

Spelling Secret

When a one-syllable word ends in a vowel followed by a consonant, double the consonant before adding ***-ing***. Example: ***pop + ing = popping***. (See the extra ***p***?)

Spelling Secret

When a verb ends in a silent ***e***, drop the ***e*** before adding ***-ing***. Example: ***drive + ing = driving***. (Notice that the ***e*** is gone!)

make + ing = ______________________

ride + ing = ______________________

leave + ing = ______________________

bake + ing = ______________________

move + ing = ______________________

No Rules Here!

(Irregular Verbs)

When it comes to irregulars, the rules fly out the window. Help students become familiar with frequently used, hard-to-spell irregular verbs.

If you spend time with a preschooler, you'll notice that he or she will make some interesting speech "mistakes." Instead of saying "We went to the beach," she might say, "We goed to the beach." Instead of "I swam for a long time," he'll say, "I swimmed for a long time." The errors are very telling; they show that the preschooler is learning the basic rule for putting verbs in the past tense and applying it to every verb he or she knows. The child does not yet realize that there are a great many exceptions to the *-ed* rule!

Your students are likely well beyond making such errors in their daily speech. But when it comes to writing, they may make similar mistakes. Once students learn a spelling rule, such as adding *-ed* to form the past tense, it can be tempting to apply that rule across the board. As part of your spelling curriculum, you'll want to pay special attention to irregular verbs, especially those that we use most frequently. In this chapter, you'll find activities to teach and reinforce the spelling of high-frequency irregular verbs.

Past-Tense Parade Board Game

Use with Kids' Pages 62–63.

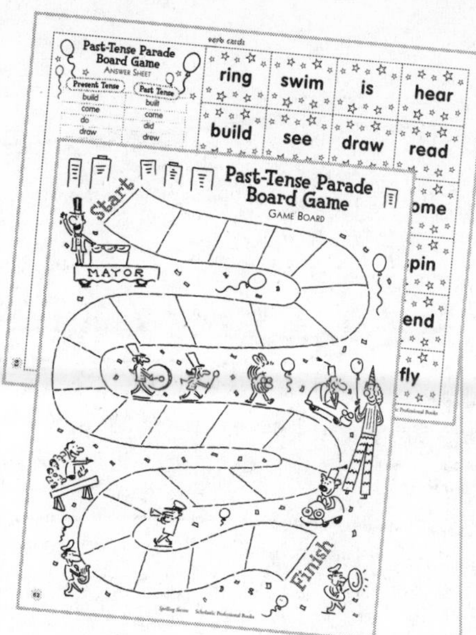

Students will get plenty of practice spelling the past-tense form of common irregular verbs by playing this easy-to-prepare board game. In the game, students draw a card with a present-tense verb and write the past tense form directly on the game board.

Spelling the past tense of irregular verbs

You Will Need

- copy of Kids' Pages 62–63 for each pair of students
- markers, colored pencils, or crayons (each pair of students needs two different colors)
- dice (one die for each pair)
- scissors

What to Do

1 Divide the class into pairs and provide each pair with a game board and a set of verb cards (if you haven't already cut apart the cards, have students do this now). Do not give out the answer sheets yet.

2 Players choose the colored pencil, marker, or crayon they will use. The two players must choose different colors and must use those colors throughout the game.

3 Have players shuffle the verb cards and place them facedown.

4 The first player rolls the die and moves to the appropriate space on the game board. The player then draws a verb card and reads the verb. He or she says and spells the past tense of the verb out loud and writes the verb in the past tense on his or her space on the game board. It is important for the player to use his or her designated color when writing the verb.

5 Player 2 follows the same directions. If player 2 happens to land on a space that has already been filled in with a verb, he or she does not draw a verb card but sits on that space until his or her next turn.

6 When both players have reached the finish line, distribute the answer sheet. Have students check the spelling of each past-tense verb they wrote on the game board. The player with the most correctly spelled verbs is the winner.

Challenge each pair of players to write a short story together featuring the past-tense irregular verbs that appear on the game board. Then have each pair share its story with the rest of the class. Because each pair will have shuffled the cards differently and drawn different verbs, you will cover many irregular verbs with this exercise.

Past-Tense Parade Board Game

GAME BOARD

Past-Tense Parade Board Game

ANSWER SHEET

Present Tense	Past Tense
build	built
come	came
do	did
draw	drew
drive	drove
fly	flew
go	went
have	had
hear	heard
is	was
keep	kept
know	knew
make	made
read	read
ring	rang
rise	rose
see	saw
send	sent
sit	sat
spin	spun
swim	swam
think	thought
wake	woke
win	won

ring	swim	is	hear
build	see	draw	read
go	do	make	come
drive	sit	have	spin
win	know	wake	send
rise	think	keep	fly

Name 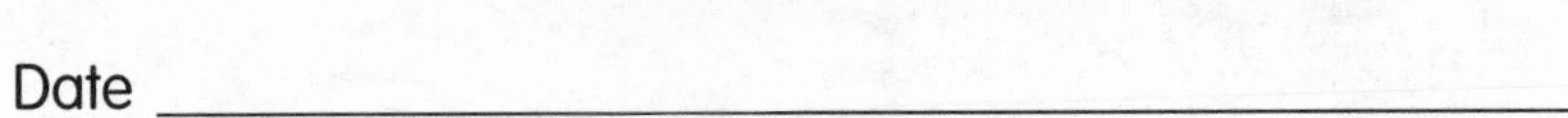

Date ______________________

Spelling irregular verbs

Spelling Skylines

Complete each sentence with a verb from the Word Box. The boxes show the shapes of the letters!

Spelling Secret
Draw boxes like the ones on this page for words you have trouble spelling. The shape and number of the boxes will help you remember the letters that make up the word.

1. We ☐☐☐☐ all day long.
2. Trevor ☐☐☐ a hole in the ground.
3. I ☐☐☐ a painting at the museum.
4. My parents ☐☐☐ me go to the movies.
5. We ☐☐☐☐ an interesting magazine.
6. Someone ☐☐☐☐ the bell.
7. The teacher ☐☐☐☐ a snowman on the board.
8. Jordan ☐☐☐☐☐☐ a toy for her puppy.
9. Simon ☐☐☐ outside after dinner.
10. The baby ☐☐☐☐☐ a tower out of blocks.

dug	**built**
ran	**let**
saw	**read**
drew	**rang**
swam	**bought**

Name ______________________________

Date ______________________________

Be a News Editor!

Eight verbs are spelled incorrectly in this news story. Find them, then use the Spelling Secret tip, right, to correct the mistakes.

Spelling Secret

When you edit someone's writing, circle a misspelled word. Then write it correctly in the margin. Here's an example:

Thomas rided rode **his horse up the hill.**

Great Apes Escape!

Two gorillas escaped from the City Zoo yesterday. The gorillas, named Harry and Lily, finded an unlocked door in their exhibit and used the door to sneak out of the zoo. The clever apes weared sunglasses and fake noses to disguise themselves as they maked their way into the downtown area.

Once downtown, Harry and Lily goed to the supermarket and buyed eight bushels of fresh bananas. "They were gorillas?" said store clerk Ima Sleepy. "I thinked they seemed a little hairy, but I didn't want to say anything."

Harry and Lily finally getted back to the zoo around 10 P.M., after taking a taxi cab on a tour of the city. According to the police, the two gorillas tryed to pay for their ride with banana peels.

Spelling Stumpers

(Spelling Aids and Strategies)

Find strategies and activities to help students face their spelling demons!

Even after studying all the rules and memorizing a multitude of exceptions, students will still face some spelling stumpers—words that give them trouble each and every time they encounter them. Some are words that you might expect to cause trouble—confusing pairs like *desert* and *dessert*, for example. Others are words that, for one reason or another, have become personal challenges to the individual student.

In this chapter you'll find some enjoyable and effective activities for tackling those tricky words. You'll also find spelling suggestions from some of the nation's top spellers—former finalists in the National Spelling Bee, sponsored by the Scripps-Howard media company. Sure, these super spellers are used to facing down words like *succedaneum* and *demarche* (the 2001 and 2000 winning words). But their tips on learning and remembering spellings of words can be applied to any word that students encounter.

Spelling study tips

Tips From Top Spellers

How can you be a super speller? Try these spelling secrets from former finalists and coaches in the National Spelling Bee!

Spell words out loud when studying. Write tricky words on index cards and post them around your house or classroom. And read everything—books, magazines, newspapers, even the dictionary!

—Sara and Stephanie Firebaugh, finalists, Indiana

Keep a spelling notebook. In it, divide words into categories. For example, you might have a section for words with troublesome endings and a section for words that come from other languages.

—April DeGideo, finalist, Pennsylvania

Make up silly sentences to help you remember tough words. For example, to remember the spelling of *separate*, say "*Sep* and *rate* are separated by an *a*." To remember the spelling of *committee*, say, "Two *m*'s, two *t*'s, and two *e*'s all sat on the committee."

—Barrie Trinkle, finalist, Washington

Play "categories" when you are riding in the car. First, choose a subject such as animals or foods. Then try to name and spell one item in that category that begins with each letter of the alphabet. Be sure to spell each word correctly! Other fun spelling games are Scrabble and Boggle.

—Peg McCarthy, spelling bee coach, Kansas

When you are reading, look up any unfamiliar words in a dictionary. Pay attention to spelling, pronunciation, and origin. Then use the word in conversation or writing as soon as possible to practice and help remember it.

—Amanda C. Goad, finalist, Virginia

Spelling tricky words

Sign-Language Spelling

Use with Kids' Page 69.

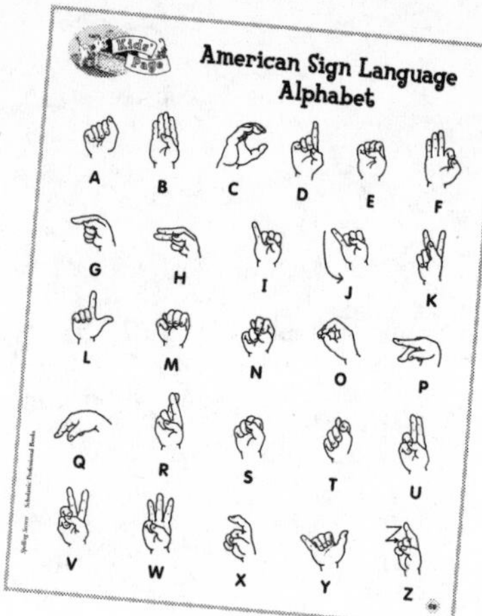

As you know, students have different styles of learning. Some children remember spelling words they have seen in print several times. For auditory learners, chanting or singing the spelling of a tough word may do the trick. Now here's a way to turn spelling into a fun physical activity for kinesthetic, or hands-on, learners! Have students use the traditional letter signs from American Sign Language to spell tough-to-remember words, and the proper spellings will be easier to recall.

To launch the activity, distribute copies of the sign-language alphabet chart on page 69. Using your own spelling list or the word wall mini-poster of commonly misspelled words on page 8, have students drill each other. One student signs the word, while the other "reads" the letter signs and names the word.

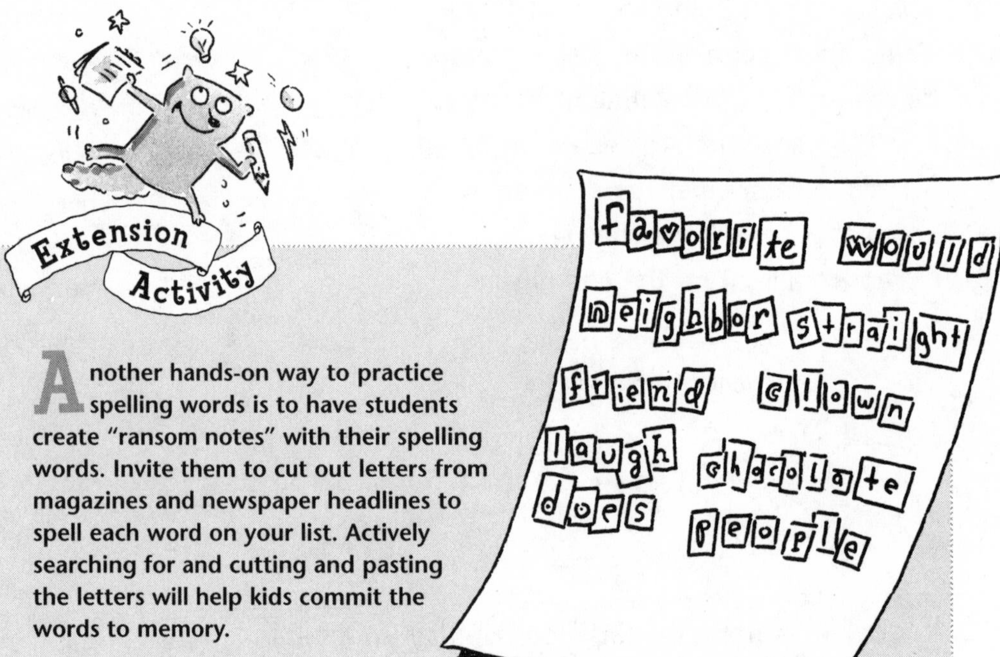

Another hands-on way to practice spelling words is to have students create "ransom notes" with their spelling words. Invite them to cut out letters from magazines and newspaper headlines to spell each word on your list. Actively searching for and cutting and pasting the letters will help kids commit the words to memory.

Kids' Page

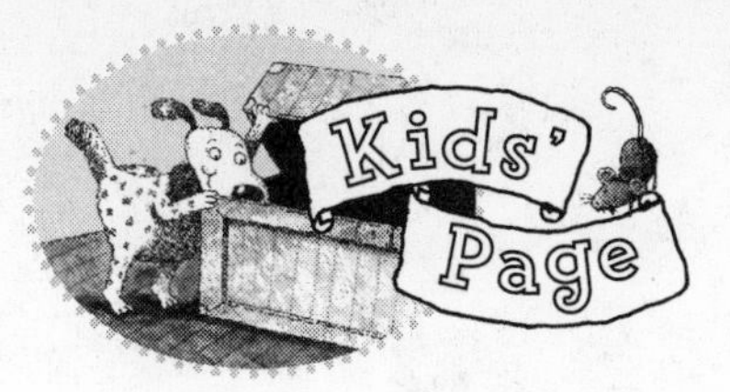

American Sign Language Alphabet

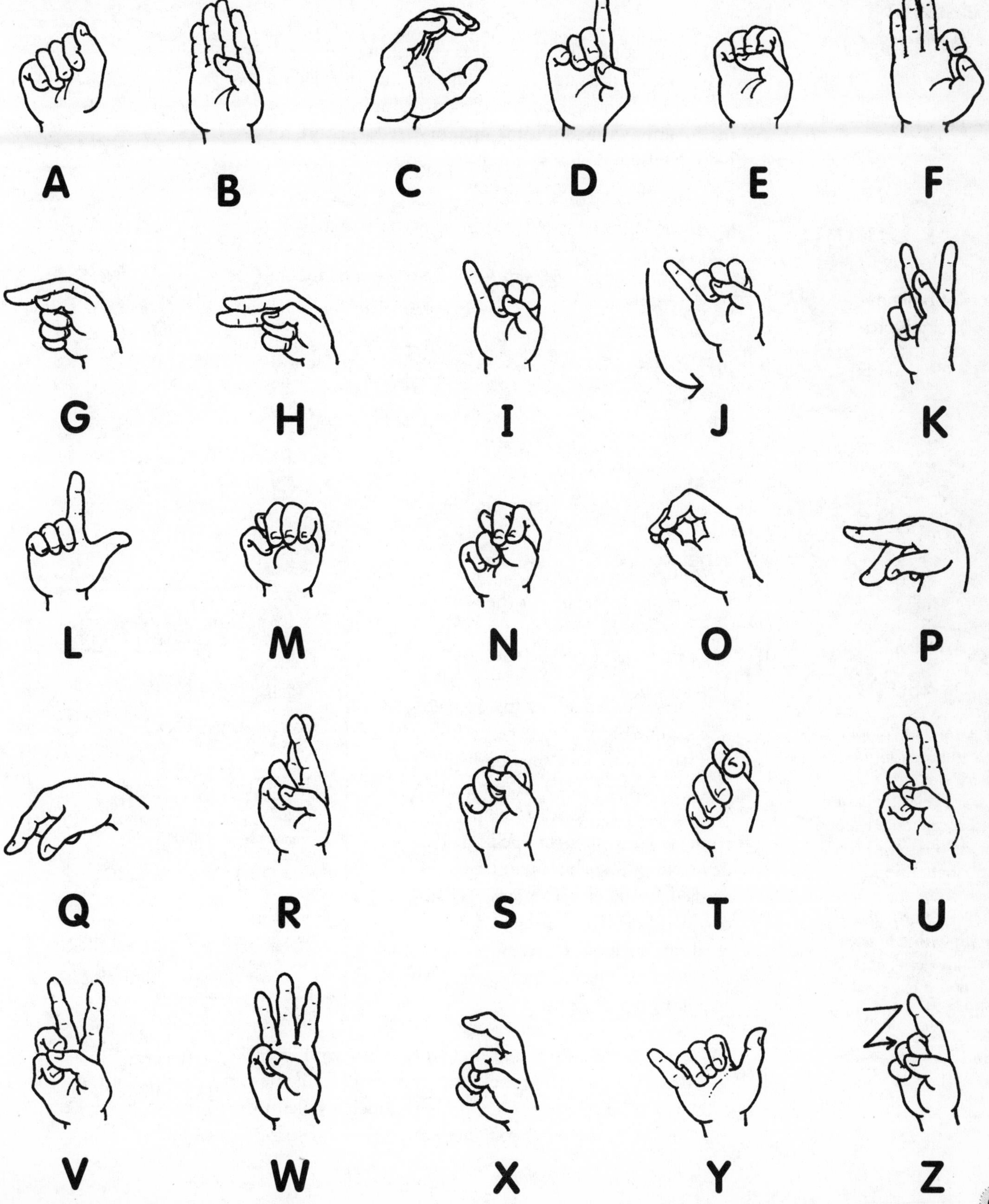
A
B
C
D
E
F
G
H
I
J
K
L
M
N
O
P
Q
R
S
T
U
V
W
X
Y
Z

Spelling tricky words

Personal Pocket Dictionary

Use with Kids' Page 71.

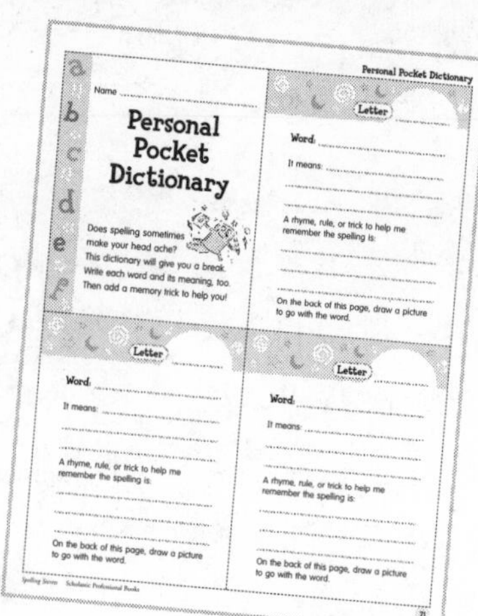

Personal Pocket Dictionary

a b c d e f

Name

Personal Pocket Dictionary

Does spelling sometimes make your head ache? This dictionary will give you a break. Write each word and its meaning, too. Then add a memory trick to help you!

Letter

Word:

It means:

A rhyme, rule, or trick to help me remember the spelling is:

On the back of this page, draw a picture to go with the word.

Many people find themselves consulting a dictionary to spell the same few words over and over again. In this activity students construct personal mini-dictionaries with a built-in "memory trick" feature to help them remember spellings for good.

You Will Need

- several copies of Kids' Page 71 for each student (the more words students want to incorporate into their dictionaries, the more copies they will need)
- scissors
- pencils
- hole punch
- string or ribbon

Instead of compiling the pages into book form, students can discard the title page and create an envelope for each letter of the alphabet. They can then store all of their spelling words that begin with *a* in their "A" envelope, and so on. If you use small, 3- by 5-inch envelopes, students can organize the envelopes in a decorated shoebox.

What to Do

1 Have students cut out the four frames on the reproducible and write their name on the cover.

2 Show students how to complete a sample dictionary page by filling in a word from your spelling list, along with the word's meaning and a simple memory device to help students remember the spelling. The device might be a rule you have studied, a mnemonic, a rap or chant, or any other trick that helps students recall the spelling. For example, you might create a page for the word *quiet* (see illustration, right).

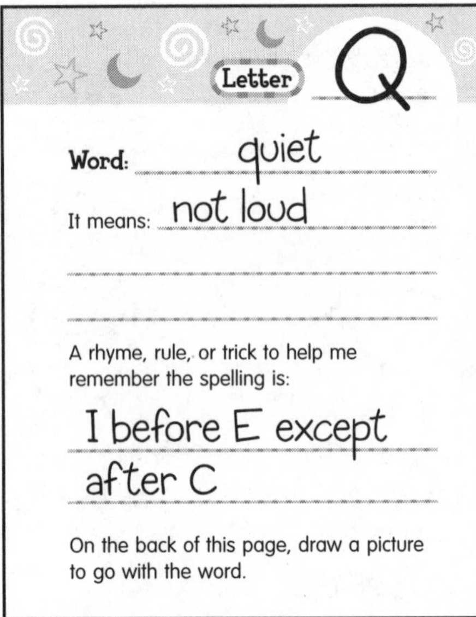

Letter Q

Word: quiet

It means: not loud

A rhyme, rule, or trick to help me remember the spelling is:

I before E except after C

On the back of this page, draw a picture to go with the word.

3 Have students create as many pages as they'd like (they can add to their dictionaries at any time). Students should put the pages in alphabetical order with the title page on top, then punch a hole in the top left corner of each page and bind the pages together with a piece of string or ribbon.

Name ________________

Personal Pocket Dictionary

Does spelling sometimes make your head ache?
This dictionary will give you a break.
Write each word and its meaning, too.
Then add a memory trick to help you!

Letter ______

Word: ______________

It means: ______________

____

____

A rhyme, rule, or trick to help me remember the spelling is:

____

____

____

On the back of this page, draw a picture to go with the word.

Letter ______

Word: ______________

It means: ______________

____

____

A rhyme, rule, or trick to help me remember the spelling is:

____

____

____

On the back of this page, draw a picture to go with the word.

Letter ______

Word: ______________

It means: ______________

____

____

A rhyme, rule, or trick to help me remember the spelling is:

____

____

____

On the back of this page, draw a picture to go with the word.

Spelling
tricky words

Spelling CPR Study Aid

Use with Kids' Pages 73–74.

Jotting down an unfamiliar word immediately after encountering it can help students remember the word's correct spelling and usage. In this activity, students construct folded-paper manipulatives to help them **C**opy, **P**ractice using, and **R**ewrite new or especially challenging spelling words. Use the manipulative to breathe new life into your spelling curriculum!

You Will Need

- double-sided copy of Kids' Pages 73–74 for each student
- scissors
- crayons or colored pencils (optional)

What to Do

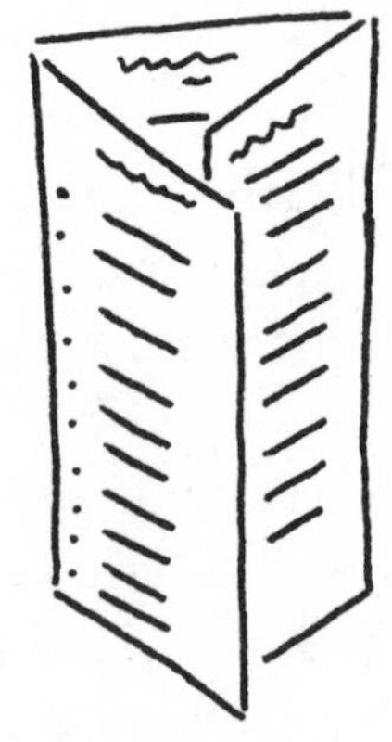

1 Have students cut out the template along the dotted lines, then fold in along the solid lines to create a narrow accordion-style trifold. The title "Spelling CPR" should appear on the front of the manipulative. Invite students to color the manipulative, if they like.

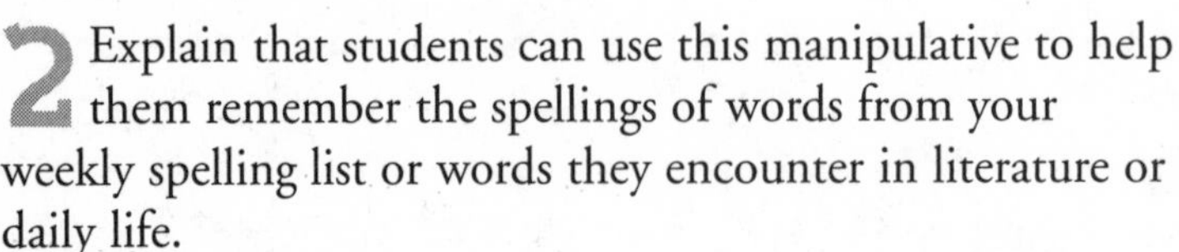

2 Explain that students can use this manipulative to help them remember the spellings of words from your weekly spelling list or words they encounter in literature or daily life.

3 Tell students to follow the instructions at the top of each section to copy, practice using, and rewrite each spelling word. They should work on one word at a time. First, students copy the word onto the front section of the manipulative. Then they open to the second section and write a sentence using the word. Finally, they turn to the last section of the manipulative and rewrite the word—without peeking at the first two sections. Because they had to write the word repeatedly and remember its spelling without glancing back at it, they are likely to remember its spelling.

Practice using the word in a sentence. Then open to the next section.

1. ______
2. ______
3. ______
4. ______
5. ______
6. ______
7. ______
8. ______
9. ______
10. ______

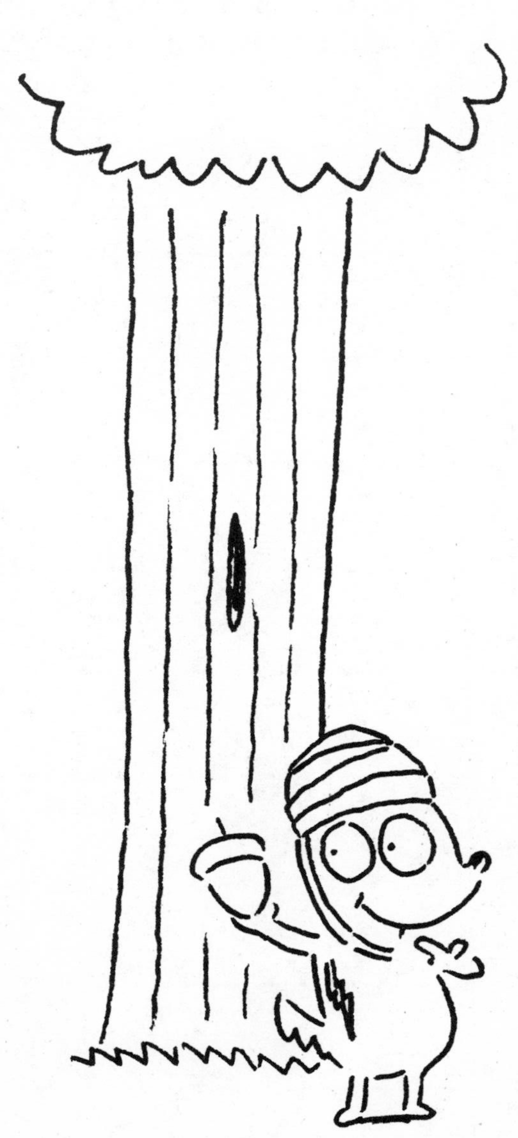

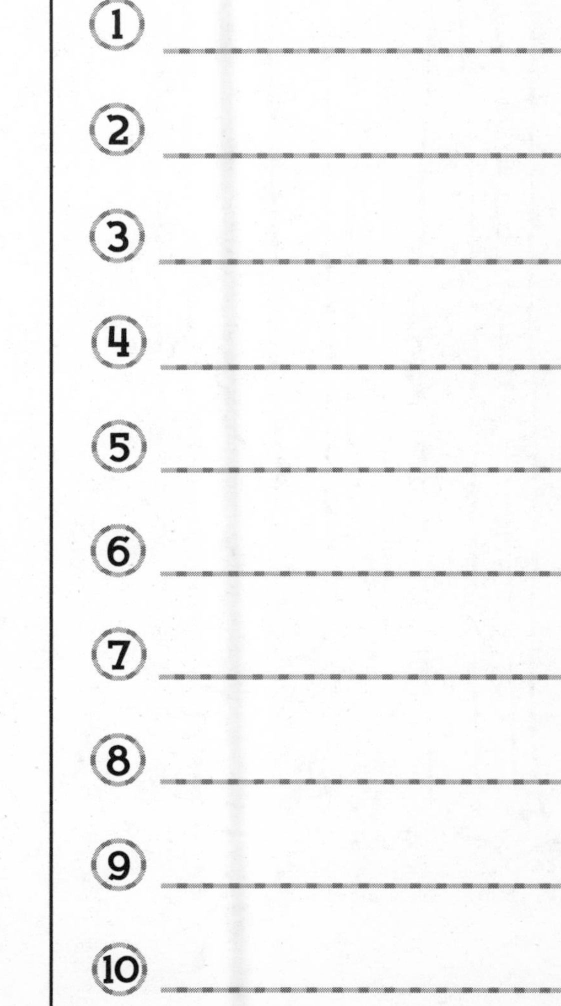

Spelling CPR

Use this tool to learn new spelling words.

First, **copy** the word below. Then open to the next section.

1. ______
2. ______
3. ______
4. ______
5. ______
6. ______
7. ______
8. ______
9. ______
10. ______

Rewrite the word without looking back at it. Then check your work. Did you spell the word correctly?

1. ______________________
2. ______________________
3. ______________________
4. ______________________
5. ______________________
6. ______________________
7. ______________________
8. ______________________
9. ______________________
10. ______________________

Focus

Spelling memory aids

Name ______________________

Date ______________________

Spelling Secret

Mnemonic devices can be as silly as you like. The important thing is that they stick in your mind!

Make a Mnemonic!

A *mnemonic* (ni-MON-ik) device is a trick that people use to remember something. You can make a mnemonic device to remember the letters in a word. Look at the example below. Then write some of your own.

Word: FRIEND

Fred
Really
Is
Earth's
Nicest
Dude

Word: DESSERT

D ______________________
E ______________________
S ______________________
S ______________________
E ______________________
R ______________________
T ______________________

Word: LAUGH

L ______________________
A ______________________
U ______________________
G ______________________
H ______________________

Word: CHOCOLATE

C ______________________
H ______________________
O ______________________
C ______________________
O ______________________
L ______________________
A ______________________
T ______________________
E ______________________

On the other side of this paper, write a mnemonic device for one of your own spelling words.

Spelling
tricky words

Confusing Words Cube

Use with Kids' Page 77.

There are certain sets of words that students (and adults!) mix up frequently. If you have ever seen a student write that he or she likes to eat brownies for *desert* or would like to visit the Sahara *Dessert*, you are already familiar with this phenomenon! These are not technically homophones because they do not sound the same, but they can be just as confusing! In this activity students create cubes that spell and define some of the most frequently mixed-up word pairs. Encourage students to display their cubes on their desks at school or at home as a ready reminder of which word to use.

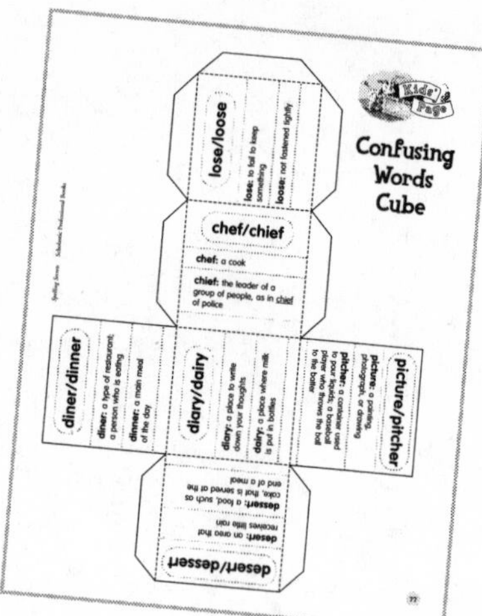

You Will Need

 copy of Kids' Page 77 for each student

 scissors

 tape or glue

What to Do

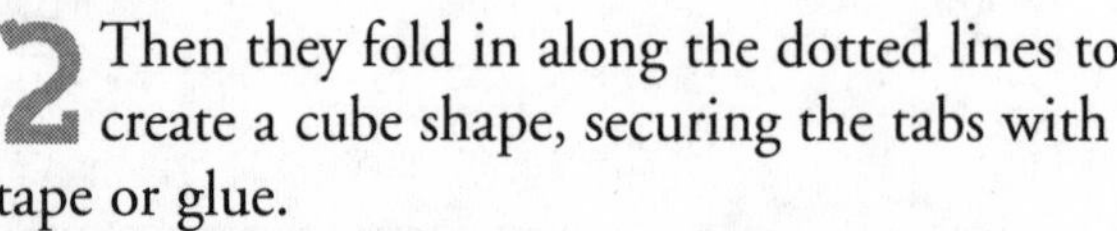

1 Distribute the reproducible and direct students to cut out the cube template along the outer solid lines.

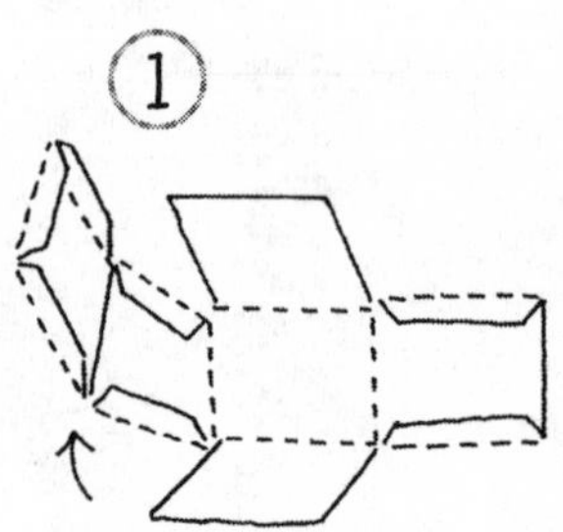

2 Then they fold in along the dotted lines to create a cube shape, securing the tabs with tape or glue.

3 Have students take turns tossing a cube and reading aloud the word pair that appears on the top of the cube. Ask students to write sentences using each of the tricky words.

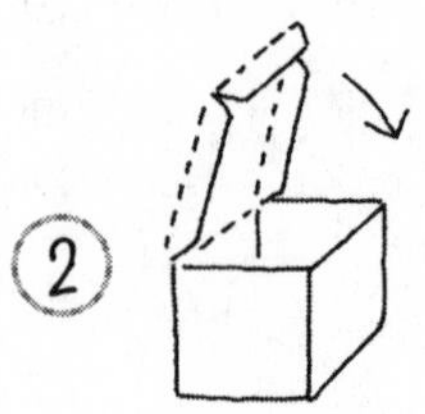

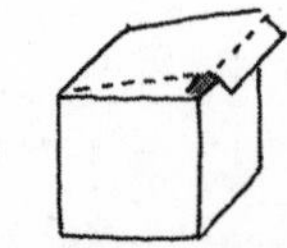

Kids' Page

Confusing Words Cube

lose/loose

lose: to fail to keep something

loose: not fastened tightly

chef/chief

chef: a cook

chief: the leader of a group of people, as in chief of police

diner/dinner

diner: a type of restaurant; a person who is eating

dinner: a main meal of the day

diary/dairy

diary: a place to write down your thoughts

dairy: a place where milk is put in bottles

picture/pitcher

picture: a painting, photograph, or drawing

pitcher: a container used to pour liquids; a baseball player who throws the ball to the batter

desert/dessert

desert: an area that receives little rain

dessert: a food, such as cake, that is served at the end of a meal

Chapter 1

The Knight's Knot (page 10): The words, in the order in which they appear in the tale, are: knit, knew, knot, knife, knight, knee, knocked, knob.

Tough Enough! (page 12): *Across:* 4. phone; 5. laugh; 6. graph; 9. photo. *Down:* 1. enough; 2. rough; 3. geography; 4. Philip; 7. tough; 8. cough.

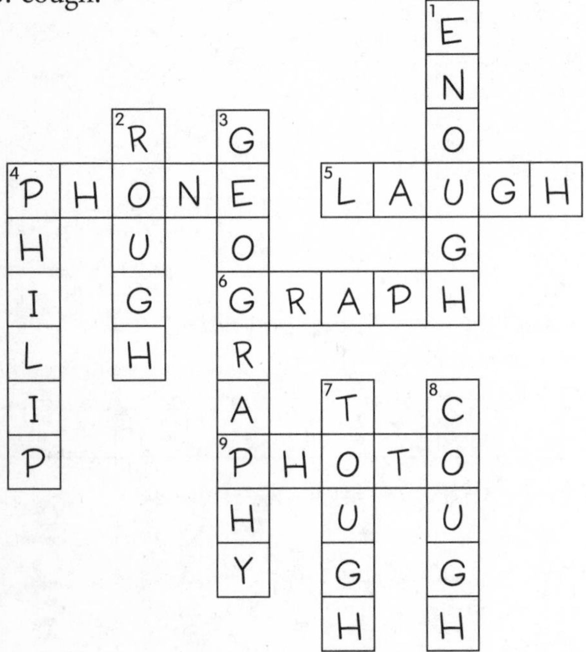

Climb Aboard! (page 17): 1. lamb; 2. climb; 3. comb; 4. numb; 5. tombstone; 6. limb. Message: "You have learned some new words; way to go! Soon you will be a spelling pro!"

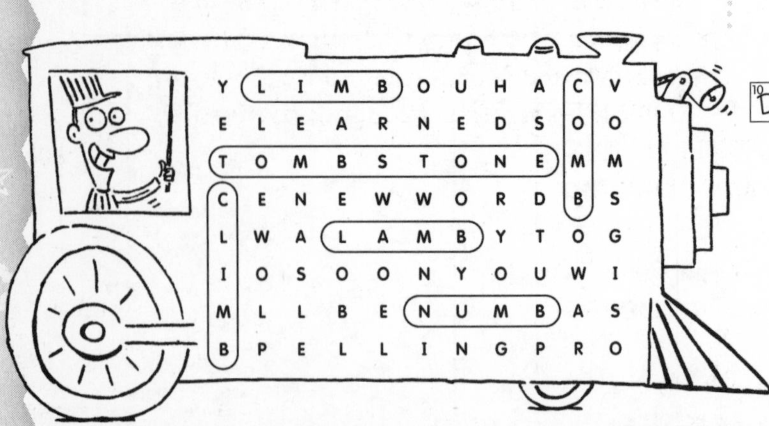

Spelling Snake (page 18): The words, in order, are: star, city, snore, scissors, son, circle, scene, silly, scientist, cider.

Chapter 2

Which Word? (page 25): 1. bear; 2. new; 3. where; 4. their; 5. bare; 6. peace; 7. wear; 8. piece; 9. knew; 10. there.

Their, They're, or There? (page 29): 1. their; 2. there; 3. they're; 4. there; 5. their, they're; 6. there; 7. there; 8. their.

Chapter 3

Build-a-Word Crossword Puzzle (page 35): *Across:* 2. cupcake; 6. fingerprint; 8. toothpaste; 9. baseball; 10. doorbell. *Down:* 1. raindrop; 3. starfish; 4. sunburn; 5. headache; 7. toolbox.

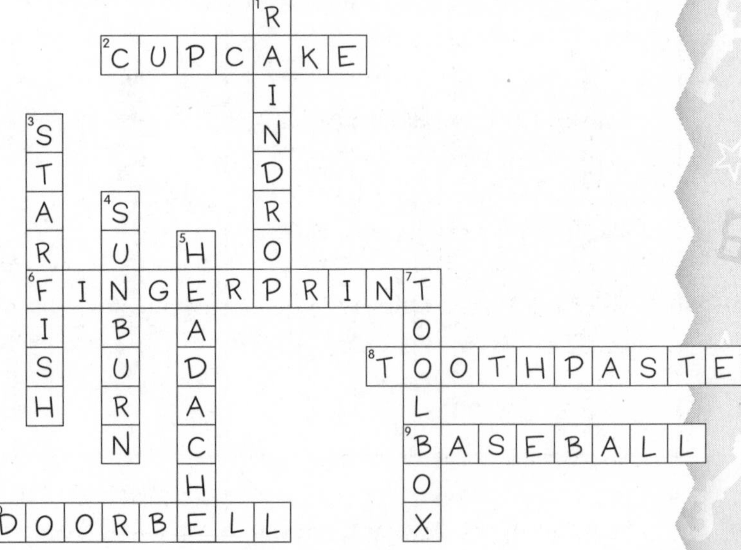

Flower Power (page 36): The flowers form the following words: airport, airline, airmail, airplane; fireplace, fireworks, firefighter, firefly; snowstorm, snowmobile, snowflake, snowball; Sunday, sunset, sunshine, sunburn.

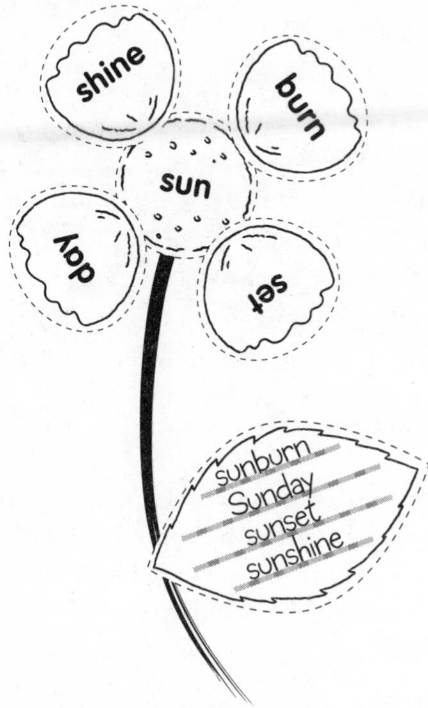

Calling All Contractions! (page 41): 1. Let's; 2. I'm; 3. We'll; 4. don't; 5. She's; 6. He'd; 7. should've; 8. What's; 9. They're; 10. couldn't. Riddle solution: "So it would not have to wait for the bus!"

The "NOT" Spot Spinner (page 42): can/can't; could/couldn't; was/wasn't; is/isn't.

Chapter 4

Sammy's Eight Days of Camping Plurals Mini-Book (page 46): Check to see that students have spelled the following plurals correctly: owls; foxes; leaves; bunnies; monkeys; flamingoes; mice.

Crack the Plurals Code! (page 50): trees; geese; wishes; skis; diaries; feet; friends; boxes; deer; keys; seas; women.

Spell-the-Past-Tense-Perfectly! Word Search (page 51): 1. walked; 2. called; 3. opened; 4. gathered; 5. used; 6. sailed; 7. printed; 8. shoveled; 9. missed; 10. decided.
Riddle solution: "On the pages of Webster's Dictionary, silly!"

G	O	N	S	D	E	C	I	D	E	D	T
A	H	W	A	L	K	E	D	E	P	D	P
T	A	G	I	E	S	U	O	F	E	M	R
H	W	E	L	B	S	T	S	L	E	I	I
E	O	P	E	N	E	D	L	E	R	S	N
R	S	D	D	I	C	A	T	I	D	S	T
E	O	N	A	R	C	Y	S	I	L	E	E
D	L	Y	S	H	O	V	E	L	E	D	D

Greetings From Camp Spelli-Melli! Past-Tense Slider (page 52): The past-tense verbs, in order, are: was; hiked; swam; sang; toasted; were; made; was; loved.

Presto Change-o! With -ing (page 59): running; stirring; setting; putting; sledding; making; riding; leaving; baking; moving.

Chapter 5

Spelling Skylines (page 64): 1. swam; 2. dug; 3. saw; 4. let; 5. read; 6. rang; 7. drew; 8. bought; 9. ran; 10. built.

Be a News Editor! (page 65): The errors and corrections are: finded (found); weared (wore); maked (made); goed (went); buyed (bought); thinked (thought); getted (got); tryed (tried).

Additional Spelling Resources

Web Sites

http://teenwriting.about.com/cs/blspellinglessons/index.htm

This site includes spelling lessons for teachers in the elementary as well as higher grades.

www.funbrain.com/spell/

This Learning Network site lets kids drill their spelling skills with a fun quiz. Click on "Easy" or "Hard" to match your students' skill level.

www.spellingbee.com

The official Scripps-Howard National Spelling Bee site offers details on the annual bee. Click on Carolyn's Corner to explore word elements, origins, and more.

Books

Best-Ever Activities for Grades 2–3: Spelling, by Joan Novelli (Scholastic, 2002) features teacher-tested activities, games, and hands-on reproducibles to help students of all learning styles master spelling strategies and rules. Includes tips for working with second-language learners and assessment ideas.

Overhead Teaching Kit: Easy Spelling Lessons for the Overhead, by Jennifer Jacobsen (Scholastic, 2002). This kit includes 12 graphic organizer transparencies that give students a visual structure for a variety of spelling skills and strategies, plus step-by-step lesson plans, reproducibles, extension ideas, and literature suggestions.

Teaching and Assessing Spelling, by Dr. Mary Jo Fresch and Aileen Wheaton (Scholastic, 2002) includes a teacher-developed assessment for determining each student's spelling knowledge along with the how-to's for teaching spelling and word study.

The Scholastic Children's Dictionary (1996) includes spelling hints, word histories, and other features to help improve spelling skills.

25 Super-Fun Spelling Games, by Nancy Jolson Leber (Scholastic, 1999) offers fun reproducible games to help kids learn the words on their spelling lists.

Writing Skills Made Fun: Capitalization, Punctuation & Spelling, by Karen Kellaher (Scholastic, 2001). Engaging reproducible games and manipulatives that teach and reinforce important skills, plus proofreading checklists, review sheets, and a colorful poster.